*Baedeker*

# Singapore

# Contents

## Nature, Culture, History
Pages 7–39

**Facts and Figures 7**
General 7 · Population 12 · Language 12 · Religion 14 · Culture 18 · State 21 · Economy 22 · Transport 25

**Famous People 28**

**History 32**

**Singapore in Quotations 37**

## Sights from A to Z
Pages 41–100

Alkaff Mansion 41
Arab Street 41
Armenian Church 41
Botanic Gardens 42
Bugis Street 43
Bukit Timah Nature Reserve 44
Changi Airport 44
Changi Beach 45
Chesed-el-Synagogue 46
Chettiars Hindu Temple 46
Chinatown 48
Chinese Chamber of Commerce 50
Clarke Quay 51
Crocodile Farm 51
East Coast Park Lagoon 52
Emerald Hill 53
Empress Place 53
Fort Canning Park 54
Fuk Tak Ch'i Temple 55
Geylang Serai 55
Hajjah Fatima Mosque 56
Haw Par Villa 56
High Street 57
Hong San See Temple 57
House of Tan Yeok Nee 58
Johor Bahru 58
Jurong Town 60
Kelongs 62

## Practical Information from A to Z
Pages 102–155

Air Travel 102 Antiques 105 Beaches 106
Boat Cruises 106 Bus Trips 107
Camping 107 Car Rental 107 Chinese Street
Opera 108 Cinema 109 Clothing 109
Conduct 109 Concerts 110 Currency 110
Customs Regulations 113 Diplomatic
Representation 113 Disabled Access 114
Drugs 114 Electricity 115 Emergency
Service 115 Events 115 Ferries 120

**Principal Sights 4**

**Plan of Singapore Mass Rapid Transport System 135**

**Useful Telephone Numbers 156**

**Index 158**

**Imprint 160**

**Large map of Singapore at end of book**

Keppel Harbour 62
Keramat Habib Noh 62
Kong Meng San Phor Kark See Temple 62
Kota Tinggi 63
Kranji War Memorial 63
Kuan Yin Temple 64
Kusu Island 64
Little India 65
MacRitchie Reservoir 66
Malacca 66
Mandai Orchid Gardens 71
Marina Bay 71
Markets 72
Merlion Park 74
Ming Village 74
Mount Faber 76
Nagore Durgha Shrine 76
National Museum 77
National Stadium 77
National University 78
Padang 78
Pasir Ris Beach Park 79
Pulau Hantu 79
Queen Elizabeth Walk 79
Raffles City 80
Raffles Hotel 80
Raffles Place 83
Saint Andrew's Cathedral 83
Saint John's Islands 83
Seletar Reservoir 84
Sentosa Island 84
Singapore River 89
Siong Lim See Monastery 90
Sisters Island 90
Sri Mariamman Hindu Temple 90
Sri Srinivassa Perumal Temple 92
Substation 92
Sultan Mosque 93
Supreme Court 93
Tang Dynasty City 94
Tanjung Pinang 95
Tan Si Chong Su Temple 95
Telok Ayer Street 95
Temple of 1000 Lights 96
Thian Hok Keng Temple 97
Turf Club 98
Van Kleef Aquarium 99
Victoria Memorial Hall and Victoria Theatre 99
Zoological Gardens 99

Folklore 120 Food and Drink 120
Getting to 124 Health Care 125 Hotels 127
Information 129 Insurance 129 Libraries 130
Lost Property 131 Measurements 131
Motoring 131 Museums 131
Newspapers 132 Nightlife 132 Opening Times 132 Parks and Nature Reserves 133
Photography 133 Post 134 Public Holidays 134 Public Transport 136
Radio and Television 137 Rail Travel 138
Religious Services 138 Restaurants 139
Shopping 143 Sightseeing 147
Souvenirs 151 Sport 151 Tailormade clothing 153 Taxis 154 Telecommunications 154 Time 154 Tipping 155
Toilets 155 Travel Agencies 155 Travel Documents 155 Weather Forecasts 155
When to Go 156 Youth Hostels 156

# The Principal Places of Tourist Interest at a Glance

| ★★ | Page |
|---|---|
| Chettiars Hindu Temple | 46 |
| Chinatown | 48 |
| Haw Par Villa | 56 |
| Johor Bahru | 58 |
| Malacca | 66 |
| Sentosa Island | 84 |
| Siong Lim See Monastery | 90 |

| ★★ | Page |
|---|---|
| Sri Mariamman Hindu Temple | 90 |
| Tanjung Pinang | 95 |
| Temple of 1000 Lights | 96 |
| Thian Hok Keng Temple | 97 |
| Zoological Gardens | 99 |

| ★ | Page |
|---|---|
| Botanic Gardens | 42 |
| Changi Airport | 44 |
| Chesed-el-Synagogue | 46 |
| Clarke Quay | 51 |
| Fort Canning Park | 54 |
| Geylang Serai | 55 |
| Hajjah Fatima Mosque | 56 |
| Hong San See Temple | 57 |
| Jurong Town | 60 |
| Keramet Habib Noh | 62 |
| Kong Meng San Phor Kark See Temple | 62 |
| Kuan Yin Temple | 64 |
| Little India | 65 |
| Mandai Orchid Gardens | 71 |

| ★ | Page |
|---|---|
| Marina Bay | 71 |
| Markets | 72 |
| Mount Faber | 76 |
| Prisoners Chapel (Changi Beach) | 46 |
| Raffles City | 80 |
| Raffles Hotel | 80 |
| Sri Srinivassa Perumal Temple | 92 |
| Sultan Mosque | 93 |
| Tang Dynasty City | 94 |
| Tan Si Chong Su Temple | 95 |
| Telok Ayer Street | 95 |
| Van Kleef Aquarium | 99 |

# Preface

This guide is one of the new generation of Baedeker guides.

Illustrated throughout in colour, they are designed to meet the needs of the modern traveller. They are quick and easy to consult, with the principal places of interest described in alphabetical order, and the information is presented in a format that is both attractive and easy to follow.

The subject of this guide is principally the island city state of Singapore, but also included are excursions to Malaysia and Indonesia.

The guide is in three parts. The first part gives a general account of Singapore, its population, language, religion, culture, state, economy, transport, famous people and history. A selection of quotations provides a transition into the second part, in which the places and features of tourist interest are described. The third part contains a variety of practical information. Both the sights and the practical information are listed in alphabetical order.

The new Baedeker guides are noted for their concentration on essentials and their convenience of use. They contain numerous specially drawn plans and colour illustrations; and at the end of the book is a large map making it easy to locate the various places described in the "A to Z" section of the guide with the help of the co-ordinates given at the head of each entry.

## How to use this book

Following the tradition established by Karl Baedeker in 1844, sights of particular interest are distinguished by either one ★ or two ★★ stars.

To make it easier to locate the various sights listed in the "A to Z" section of the Guide, their co-ordinates on the large map of Singapore are shown in red at the head of each entry.

Only a selection of hotels, restaurants and shops can be given: no reflection is implied, therefore, on establishments not included.

The symbol ⓘ on a town plan indicates the local tourist office from which further information can be obtained. The post-horn symbol indicates a post office.

In a time of rapid change it is difficult to ensure that all the information given is entirely accurate and up to date, and the possibility of error can never be completely eliminated. Although the publishers can accept no responsibility for inaccuracies and omissions, they are always grateful for corrections and suggestions for improvement.

# Facts and Figures

Merlion coat of arms of the Republic of Singapore

## General

Singapore – officially the Republic of Singapore – is an independent city state lying off the southern tip of the Malacca peninsula in an exceptionally favourable position, both strategically and economically.

The area of the island state includes the 587sq.km/226sq. miles of the main island of Singapore and the 54 smaller islands. Its geographical situation is 1°09' and 1°29' north of the Equator and 103°38' and 104°06' east. It is only 136.8km/85 miles from the Equator.

In the west Singapore is washed by the Straits of Malacca and the South China Sea, part of the Indian Ocean. It is connected to the mainland, the neighbouring state of Malaysia, by road and rail links along the 1km/½mile-long Johore Causeway.

Geographical states

The immediate neighbouring state in the north is the elective monarchy of Malaysia, to which Singapore belonged until 1965. Both are separated by the Selat Johor (=Johore Strait). West of Singapore, beyond the Straits of Malacca, which are only 75km/47 miles wide at this point, is the island of Sumatra, belonging to Indonesia. To the east of Singapore is the island of Kalimantan (Borneo), also part of Malaysia.

Neighbouring states

The city of Singapore covers a total area of 622.6sq.km/240sq. miles. The main island is 570.4sq.km/220sq.miles and just under one half is

Area

◀ *Skyscrapers by the Singapore River*

General

## General

built-up; the longest distances are from east to west 42km/26 miles, from north to south 23km/14 miles and the coastline measures about 135.7km/84 miles.

The main island consists of undulating granite hills which reach a maximum height of 163m/534ft. To the south and east they give way to almost flat alluvial land; the south-west is a stratified zone. In the coastal areas (partly mangroves) new land is constantly being created through the process of deposition.

Topography

Inland there are some reservoirs and small lakes. The first trading port was established on the Singapore River in the 19th c.

The name Singapore (Malay Singapura, Chinese Xinjiapo) is derived from "Singa" (= lion) and "pura" (= town).

Name and significance

The "City of Singapore" which occupies about a sixth of the main island is the capital of the island state.

Capital

The capital and the smaller urban and rural settlements are, for the main part, centrally administered. The smallest political units are the electoral constituencies with extra-parliamentary Citizen Consultative Committees appointed by the administration.

Administration

The climate of Singapore is tropical, usually oppressively close and muggy. The humidity levels occasionally reach 96% during the night and about 65% during the day, on average it is 85%.

Climate

| Climatic table<br>Month | Rainfall amounts in mm | Days with rain | Average temp. in °C | Days of sunshine | Relative humidity in % | Stormy days |
|---|---|---|---|---|---|---|
| January | 194 | 12 | 25.5 | 5.5 | 84 | 5 |
| February | 182 | 10 | 26.1 | 6.1 | 83 | 8 |
| March | 173 | 11 | 26.5 | 6.3 | 83 | 14 |
| April | 138 | 12 | 26.9 | 5.8 | 86 | 15 |
| May | 160 | 13 | 27.1 | 5.7 | 86 | 15 |
| June | 154 | 11 | 27.1 | 5.7 | 85 | 13 |
| July | 133 | 12 | 26.8 | 6.0 | 84 | 11 |
| August | 148 | 12 | 26.7 | 5.7 | 85 | 13 |
| September | 144 | 11 | 26.6 | 5.3 | 85 | 14 |
| October | 181 | 13 | 26.5 | 5.0 | 86 | 15 |
| November | 243 | 17 | 26.0 | 4.2 | 88 | 15 |
| December | 311 | 18 | 25.5 | 4.4 | 89 | 12 |
| Year | 2161 | 152 | 26.4 | 5.5 | 85 | 150 |

The temperatures are also generally high and do not fall much at night. The highest temperatures recorded are about 31°C, the lowest 24°C, the annual average temperature is 26.6°C.

Singapore has no clearly defined wet and dry periods; but most rainfall is during the north-east monsoon (from November to January); annual amount totals almost 2400mm.

Throughout the whole year there are sudden and often heavy downpours, but usually only of short duration.

Singapore normally is unaffected by tropical whirlwinds such as typhoons owing to its position close to the equator. The wind can be very strong especially during heavy storms.

Despite the tropical-maritime weather conditions most of the rain forest typical of this region has been swallowed up for development as recreational and building land. Only 19% of the total area is used agriculturally; a good 2000ha/809 acres of the main island are wooded.

Flora

**General**

## Population

**Fauna**

The larger mammals which once lived here – tigers, bears, stags, deer or wild boar – have died out. Smaller mammals such as wild cats, flying squirrels and various species of small monkeys are still to be found. There are about 100 species of birds and 400 types of butterfly together with a relatively large number of reptiles, especially lizards and snakes (some poisonous).

# Population

**Population growth**

Like other Asian cities (e.g. Hong Kong or Bangkok) Singapore has become a melting pot for the most varied ethnic groups. When Sir Stamford Raffles acquired the land of Singapore for the British East India Company in 1819 it was inhabited only by a handful of Malay fishermen. To promote its development as a commercial centre the Company brought in coolies from South China; under British colonial rule Indians and Ceylonese came to Singapore. Immigrants came and are still coming from neighbouring Malaysia hoping to find economic prosperity. Providing that they are either willing to learn or else have a good education or training they are welcomed by this prospering city state. Since the mid-Eighties a limited number of Vietnamese refugees have been admitted.

**Population size**

According to the last census in 1980 there were 2.41 million inhabitants. The population of Singapore in 1992 numbered about 3 million with an annual growth rate of 1.3%. Although the total area of Singapore has been increased in recent years by land reclamation and deposition the average population density is 4818 inhabitants per sq.km (in the 8 sq.km. of the "Central City Area" it is 20,000 per sq.km), among the highest in the world.

**Population growth**

For political and economic reasons the government is encouraging population growth and in 1988 lifted the strict birth control laws which were previously in force. Now a family with three instead of two children is desirable in order to reach the planned goal of 4 million people. Families with three or more children receive considerable tax advantages (child benefit, tax allowance for the non-working wife, special tax reduction of 20,000 S-$ for the fourth child).

**Population structure**

The heterogeneous ethnic population of Singapore comprises 76.1% Chinese, 15.1% Malay (chiefly in the rural kampongs), 6.5% Indian, Pakistani, Bangladeshi and Ceylonese (from Sri Lanka) and 2.3% Eurasian, Jewish, Armenian, Arab, Vietnamese and other tiny minorities. The numerically largest group are the 25–35 year olds (about 22%).

**Life expectancy**

The present life expectancy for men in Singapore is 70 years, for women 76 years.

**Living standards**

85% of the population live in state-built houses, most of which are now owner-occupied. More than three-quarter of all Singaporeans live in satellite towns. In 1960 the Housing and Development Board was established to improve the quality of life, promoting settlement on the outskirts of the city.

# Language

**National language**

The national language of Singapore is Malay but it is rarely spoken in public. In addition Chinese (Mandarin), which has been heavily pro-

**Language**

*A society in which racial harmony is taken for granted*

moted in recent years, and South Indian Tamil are recognised as official languages. English is the administrative language. But recently the government has been promoting standard Chinese as the official language. The promotion of Mandarin is intended to absorb the variety of Chinese dialects and steer the class thinking, prevalent in Chinese circles, towards a national identity. It should also reflect Chinese culture, acting as a counterbalance to the Westernisation which comes with the English language.

Debates in Parliament take place in all four languages with English and Mandarin dominating. The minutes of meetings are recorded only in English.

Teaching in schools from secondary level upwards takes place in English and Mandarin.

### Religion

**Languages and dialects**

The Chinese population living in Singapore speak the dialects of their original provinces (Hokkien, Teotchu, Canton, Hakka, Hainan among others). The Indians, who constitute the third largest group, apart from Tamil, speak Telegu, Malayalam, Punjabi, Hindi and Bengali.

**Chinese writing**

The development of Chinese writing with its 50,000 or more characters is one of the major cultural achievements of world history. Chinese belongs to the family of Sino-Tibetan languages, similar to the hieroglyphics of the Egyptians or Babylonians whereby symbols or pictorial representations were used to describe an object, an action or behaviour. The first precursors of the writing which is still used today are more than 4000 years old. From these very simple characters modern Chinese developed over thousands of years.

**Characters**

It was usually possible to tell what the early characters meant. But these characters have virtually nothing in common with those of today, which have become more abstracted and altered with regular usage. Basically they consist of a sign which carries the meaning and another which determines the pronunciation. Although there are numerous dialects which in some circumstances deviate considerably from standard Mandarin the characters are uniform. This means that all Chinese are at least able to communicate in written form.

Of the 50,000 or so characters an academic will know about 7000, while 2000 to 4000 suffice for everyday usage.

**Everyday writing**

A reform of colloquial writing begun in the Fifties brought about a relative simplification with about 1000 characters and resulted in the so-called Pinyin transcription which uses Latin letters. This script which has 20 consonants and six vowels was officially introduced in 1979 and chiefly facilitates contact with non-Chinese; it is also taught in schools. Other reforms intended to make it easier to learn Chinese are planned.

On the steets of Singapore Chinese characters and English signs are equally represented.

**Everyday language**

About 420 monosyllabic words or symbols determine the pronunciation most of which undergo four different stress patterns resulting in a completely different meaning (See Practical Information, Language). But even the correct pronunciation does not prevent a foreigner from being recognised as such. Writing and language are indivisible from the Chinese way of thinking.

## Religion

**General**

Singapore's ethnic variey is reflected in its religious diversity; freedom of religious belief and practice is guaranteed by the constitution.

The most important religions are Buddhism and Taoism (56%), Sunny Islams (16%), Christianity (10%) and Hinduism (4%), but the various ethnic minorities (Confucians, Jews, Sikhs and others) also practise their faith in their own places of worship.

The various denominations are represented on a joint committee (Interreligious Organisation) which advises the government on questions of religious harmony

Ecumenical activities in the widest sense, with the participation of all the religious communities, are taken as a matter of course in Singapore. However, they cannot conceal the hidden tensions between the religions which are stirred up mainly by the evangelical Christian religious communities. Parliament passed a "law of religious harmony" forbidding Muslims from proselytising and the religions from having any influence in politics.

*Buddhist monks discuss a point of doctrine* ▶

## Religion

### Buddhism

More than half of the population in Singapore are Buddhist. By far the majority of them are followers of Mahayana Buddhism believing in the teaching of the "Greater Vehicle". Hinayana Buddhism, the second stream of belief (the teaching of the "Little Vehicle"), is of little significance in Singapore as the "Greater Vehicle" ressembles the Chinese mentality more closely. The founder of the religion Budhha himself is worshipped but not prayed to.

### Siddharta Gautama (Buddha)

Siddharta Buddha (the name comes from Sanskrit and means "Enlightener") was born about 563 B.C. the son of a rich landowner (who called himself king and whose children grew up as members of a noble family named Sakya) in Nepal at the foot of the Himalayas under the name of Siddharta Gautama. Although the luxury of his parental home was formative in his early years Siddharta encountered human suffering on three occasions when he met an old man, a sick man and a dead man one after the other. On a fourth journey he met a hermit who gave the thirty-year old the incentive to give up his former way of life and to search for the meaning of human existence as an itinerant ascetic. Legend illustrates how seriously he took his decision for a son was born to him on his day of departure.

Following intense meditation, through which he searched for a balance between excess and asceticism, during his thirty-fifth year after seven years of wandering, he reached the stage of Enlightenment under a pipal tree by the small Indian river Nerajara as he went through the four stages of contemplation. The Four Holy Truths, "Suffering", the "Cause of Suffering", the "Salvation from Suffering" and "The Way to End Suffering", are the principles of his first sermon which he gave in the small Indian town of Benares.

Just three months after this sermon the number of his followers reached sixty, he sent them away into the country with the words "take the message of friendship to everyone and let no two of you take the same path!" For the forty-five years which follow he travelled throughout India preaching his teachings of the "Wheel of Suffering" (dharmacakrapravartana). He survived the attacks on his life by his cousin Devadatta who had turned against him by employing all the force of his compassionate love towards an elephant which had been incited to charge him. While Buddhist tradition is based on Buddha, through his death in 543 B.C., entering into Nirvana, a stage that releases all creatures on earth from the eternal cycle of rebirth, history records his death as 480 or 470 B.C. The year 543 is, however, important in the Buddhist calendar.

### Principles

The principles of Buddhism come from the Hindu religion, from which it took the concept of karma, the invincible cosmic law. Karma means the sum of all good and evil actions in former existences which are regularly atoned for in the rebirth. Good deeds count for so much that they can be rewarded in the next life with a better existence. The cycle is relentless, according to tradition Buddha himself is said to have completed 500 life-cycles in various forms. The cycle can – to put it simply – be influenced by every individual to the extent by which he devotes his own life to the principles of belief laid down by Buddha.

The difference between Mayahana and Hinayana Buddhism lies in the possibility of breaking through the cycle of birth–death–rebirth. Whereas Hinayana Buddhism states that every believer must achieve this without any kind of help, Mahayana Buddhism, which dates from 1st and 2nd c. A.D., recognises the Bodhisattvas. These are people who have already attained the stage of Enlightenment, but are still on earth (unrecognised) in order to show other people the "Eightfold Path of Acknowledgement" and through this the path to Nirvana. Buddha himself was a Bodhisattva after his 500 lives, before he finally went into Nirvana.

# Religion

## Confucianism

The influence and effect of Confucius ("Master K'Ung", 551–479 B.C. on Chinese culture is important. His teachings are based on the religious idea that correct behaviour can lead to harmony and eternal world order. This behaviour consists of truth towards oneself and others, selflessness, humanity, honesty, propriety, wisdom and sincerity. For China (and East Asia) the aristocratic political teachings and ethics of Confucianism were the definitive influence for many centuries from the Han dynasty (206 B.C. to A.D. 220). Piety was the cornerstone of family life and the state. The "Five Relationships" between prince and servant, father and son, husband and wife, older and younger brother, friend and friend were defined by the virtues of human love, justice and deference. These were expressed in the respect for what is inherited, rites and music and go beyond death (ancestor worship).

The ethical principles of Confucius have retained their validity and significance in lively debate until the present day. In contrast with Buddhism (with which Confucianism has basic ideas in common) and Christianity, Confucianism and Taoism founded by Lao-Tzu did not develop into world religions but remained teachings which for a long time were unknown outside of their country of origin.

## Taoism

The philosophy of Taoism arose in the 4th and 3rd c. B.C. among the speculation in Chinese philosophy about the origins of the world ("Tao"). Taoism as a religion is different, its followers seek to extend their life expectancy and achieve immortality of the body through meditation, dietics, alchemy, gymnastics and sexual practices. Since the 2nd c. A.D. at the latest there have been established cultural forms which are in competition with more advanced forms of Buddhism. The present day Vulgar Taoism is more a reconciliatory system of popular belief in which some gods of the older Taoism still survive. Philosophical Taoism on the other hand found supporters in the upper classes until quite recently and at times had a powerful influence on poetry.

## Lao-Tze

Through later Taoism the life of the philosopher Lao-Tze ("Ancient Master", 4th–3rd c. B.C.?) became legendary. Supposedly Lao-Tze did not die but only moved west over the mountains. On the way he left the book of Tao teachings to the guardian of the border pass. Its 81 short sections focus on "Tao" (origin of the world) and its living force ("Te") which the initiated can create by deep comtemplation of the "Tao". Harmony can only be achieved by non-intervention (Chinese: "wu wei") and keeping one's distance from the world. The peculiar combination of depth of thought and linguistic simplicity has resulted in 130 translations in the West of the best known work of Chinese philosophical literature.

## Yin and Yang

Part of the spiritual legacy since the 5th/3rd c. B.C. have been the teachings of the cosmological principles of Yin and Yang (Chinese: "dark" and "light"), which are attributed to all beings. Yin and Yang symbolise two complementary but independent forces which are in constant motion in our universe. Both are understood to be mutually attractive forces of an indivisible whole which, at the point where they come together, display the properties of their opposite. They do not represent cause and effect, but rather sound and echo or light and shade. Yin corresponds to the feminine (negativity, earth, compliance, unreality, passivity, goodness), Yang to the masculine (positivity, sun, determination, reality, activity). Yin and Yang are also important in Chinese medicine and alchemy.

## Superstition

As in all Asian religions superstition plays an important part in Confucianism and Taoism. One of the unusual practices followed in Singapore, for example, is calling upon the services of a Feng Shui expert (literally translated as "wind and water") when building a house or moving into a new one. He uses astrological charts based on the

**Culture**

*Lucky numberplate (e.g. 6, 8) – much prized in Singapore*

teaching of Yin and Yang to work out the "forces of the elements" (wind, water, sky, earth, streams and sun rays) and thereby decides on the most favourable position for the house or flat. Following his advice should, according to deeply-rooted belief, bring wealth and happiness.

Feng Shui experts are among the best paid men in Singapore and are often fully booked for years in advance. Even repected firms (especially those which seek to impress their Chinese colleagues) number among their clients. The Feng Shui expert does not always advise building a new house or moving into a new flat. Sometimes an octagonal mirror in front of the window or statues of lions in front of the door or keeping fish in the house (black fish guard against the devil, gold fish bring good luck) will suffice.

Certain lucky numbers or combinations of numbers (3, 6, 8 in particular) symbolise good luck to the Chinese. Car number plates with such combinations are much sought after.

**Other religions**

Other religions practised in Singapore are Islam (Sunny 350,000 followers) and Hinduism (120,000). There about 1000 members of the Jewish community.

**Christianity**

About 500,000 practise the Christian faith – Roman Catholic and Protestant – of whom 300,000 are Singaporeans. Both churches have their own kindergartens, first and middle schools together with their respective colleges.

# Culture

**General**

Singapore's cultural scene shows a mingling of elements in accord with ethnic variety. The individual elements, however, are not com

# Culture

bined but reflect the separateness of the Chinese, Indian and Malay communities. A unified national culture is still in the process of emerging. Conditioned as it is by the developing homogenisation based on the English language, it displays strongly Western characteristics. The philosophical heritage of the traditional cultures is intermingled with Western values, with the objective of achieving a national identity which transcends ethnic and community boundaries. This objective comes up against the problem, however, that the population, which is mainly Chinese in origin, nurtures and defends its Confucian traditions. As a result all attempts to create a single Singaporean identity are subtly undermined.

The Ministry of Community Development is anxious to arouse and stimulate a natural cultural consciousness: no easy matter in a society which thinks mainly in materialistic terms. A foundation seeks to promote individual artists and international cultural exchange.

## Education system

Although there is no compulsory schooling in Singapore close on 90% of all children and adolescents between six and seventeen attend school. Attendance at Primary School (six to eight years) is free: during the first three years there is freedom of choice over which language the child is taught in. The next stage is Secondary School (four to five years) with English and Chinese (Mandarin) as the languages of instruction. Before going on to university a two year course at Junior College is obligatory.

School system

Alongside numerous local school institutions there are many international and foreign schools including several British and one American, one each Armenian, Japanese, French, Swiss and German.

In 1980 the University of Singapore, which dates back to the King Edward VII College of Medicine (founded in 1905) and Raffles College (opened in 1929), was amalgamated with the Chinese Nanyang University to form the new National University of Singapore where English is the main language of instruction. It has eight faculties (natural sciences, medicine, dentistry, law, business studies, engineering, architecture and building, arts and social sciences) and some affiliated specialist institutes (including medical research, languages and management). The teaching staff is international with the present student population numbering 14,000.

Universities and colleges

Other well known colleges are the former "Nanyang Technological Institute", the "Seameo Regional Language Centre" (language academy), the "Singapore Polytechnic" and the "Ngee Ann Polytechnic". In addition Singapore is planning to establish an "Open University".

The main emphasis of academic education lies in the fields of mathematics, information technology, technology, engineering, languages, business studies and world trade.

Despite all efforts the government of Singapore has not succeeded in reducing the numbers unable to read and write. In 1985 it was around 13.9% (among women more than 21%) and remains only slightly below that figure today.

Illiteracy

The National Library has more than 2.7 million books, of which 1.5 million are in English, 740,000 in Chinese, 310,000 in Malay and the rest in Tamil and other European languages.

Libraries and archives

In addition the library has a large collection of audio recordings, microfilm, microfiche and audio-visual material as well as maps, musical recordings, works in Braille and large print.

The National Archives are also well stocked with a rich collection of Singapore records (much on microfilm or microfiche) and extensive photographic material.

**Culture**

In 1979 the Ministy of Culture began to build up in its Oral History Unit a library of recordings of personal accounts relating to the history of Singapore.

The National University of Singapore has one of the largest libraries in South-East Asia, with more than 700,000 books, periodicals, specialist journals and microfilms.

## Art

Literature

The modern literature of Singapore is of a high standard, especially its poetry. It is chiefly concerned with the social conflict between the generation of immigrants and modern youth and the massive process of radical change in a rapidly evolving society. Critical resistance in lyric form also exists against the "engineered educational democracy" of the state's founder Lee Kuan Yew, which has been adhered to by his successors.

Orchestra

Singapore has only one professional orchestra, the Singapore Symphony Orchestra (SSO), founded in 1979, which receives funds from the government. It has a strength of 70 musicians, just under half of whom are Europeans. It is planned to bring in more musicians born in Singapore who are at present studying at conservatories abroad.

The orchestra performs regularly at the Victoria Memorial Hall.

Ballet

Singapore has had its own ballet ensemble since 1987.

Theatre

The oldest theatre in Singapore is the Victoria Theatre, which was opened in 1862. In 1963 the National Theatre, with seating for 3420, was opened. Both theatres put on productions in English by visiting companies as well as local productions with amateur companies.

There is also a varied programme of traditional theatre, genuine folk plays, Indian dance dramas, Chinese operas and pop events.

*The Singapore Symphony Orchestra, Singapore's only professional orchestra*

Other venues for dramatic performances are the People's Theatre in the Kreta Ayer Complex, the auditorium of the Congress Hall, the Cultural Theatre of Singapore, the auditorium of the Development Bank, the Modern Drama centre and the small theatre in the National Museum.

Also of considerable interest are the small private theatres, such as "Act 3" (Cairnhill Road) or "Substation" (Armenian Road) which have an extensive artistically acclaimed repertoire.

Since 1986 the Singapore Festival of Arts which lasts several weeks has taken place every two years. The main attractions are the famous international groups and artists but local productions are becoming increasingly popular. The visitor can see Western and Asian classics together with modern art and folklore. Equally noteworthy is the bi-annual international film festival.

Art festival
Film festival

## State

The Republic of Singapore – Malay Repablik Singapura, Chinese Xinjiapo Gonghegno – is a city state, with a President as head of state.

State form

The Constitution resembles the British constitution yet is different. It is called an "engineered" or "educational democracy". The state, or at least its guardians, are omnipresent, intruding to considerable degree into the private life of the citizen.

Constitution

The protection of the various minorities in Singapore is laid down in the constitution. They are entitled to maintain their ethnic and cultural independence and yet still be fully integrated into society.

National flag

Coat of arms

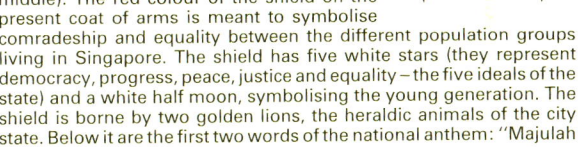

The coat of arms of Singapore was accepted by the National Assembly on 11 November 1959, before its independence from Great Britain and – later – from the Malaysian Confederation. It replaced the old coat of arms which was introduced in 1950 (a red capstan on a white background with Tudor crown in the middle). The red colour of the shield on the present coat of arms is meant to symbolise comradeship and equality between the different population groups living in Singapore. The shield has five white stars (they represent democracy, progress, peace, justice and equality – the five ideals of the state) and a white half moon, symbolising the young generation. The shield is borne by two golden lions, the heraldic animals of the city state. Below it are the first two words of the national anthem: "Majulah Singapura" (= "Forwards Singapore").

International Identification Plate

The words "Majulah Singapura" are also the motto of Singapore. The government frequently employs the slogan "One people – one nation – one Singapore" to encourage people to work together towards unity and prosperity and create the feeling of belonging together among the many different races living in Singapore.

State's motto/
State slogan

The president has only been elected by the people of Singapore since 1993. He has limited executive powers and can influence the decisions of the government in matters such as finance.

President

To further the integration of people from different races and backgrounds a presidential council of 20 members was established. Half of the members are appointed for life the others are elected every three years.

Presidential Council

The government consists of the prime minister and eleven departmental ministers (defence, national development, education, environment, communications and information, home affairs and justice,

Government

## Economy

*Victoria Memorial Hall and Raffles Statue*

*Skyscrapers dominate the Singapore skyline*

foreign affairs, finance, employment, trade and industry, health). The government is answerable to Parliament. Since independence from British colonial rule in 1963 the government has, without interruption, been formed from the ranks of the PAP (People's Action Party).

Parliament
The single chamber parliament comprises 81 deputies who because of universal suffrage are elected by the people. The period of office of parliament and the cabinet is five years.
In the last elections in 1991 the People's Action Party won 77 out of the 81 seats, although half of the voters did not vote for the PAP – a result of the British first-past-the-post system.

Parties
The system of political parties in Singapore only appears diverse. The only party which has ever really been of any significance is the PAP, which has nearly all the seats in Parliament. There is no real oppostion, the parties are even divided among themselves.

Conscription
Right to vote
Universal conscription exists in Singapore and all citizens over 21 must vote. The age for eligibility to political office is 35.

International membership
The Republic of Singapore is a member of the Commonwealth of Nations, the United Nations (since 1965), member of the Colombo Plan and a founder member of the ASEAN association founded in 1967, whose aim was the promotion of regional co-operation in economic, social and cultural areas to consolidate peace in South-East Asia.

## Economy

A world commercial centre
For 140 years Singapore was the principal British commercial centre on the shipping route between Canton (China) and Calcutta (India). About the turn of the century it became the marketing centre for natural rubber and tin from Malaysia.

# Economy

Since achieving independence in 1959 it has developed into the most modern industrial, commercial and banking centre in South-East Asia. Nowadays it is one of the "four little tigers" which in economic terms means the fast-developing nations of Asia with the strongest economies; South Korea, Taiwan, Hong Kong and Singapore.

The economy of Singapore is based primarily upon significant investment from abroad. Leading Japanese, American and European firms use the island republic as their production centre for the Far East and South-East Asia. Singapore has become the high-tech shop window for this part of the world. Preference is given to export-orientated industries.

The gross national product for 1991 at about 24,000 S-$ is the second highest in Asia (Japan has the highest). The real growth in 1991 was 6.7%, but dropped the following year to 5.6%. It is expected to rise again to over 6%.

*Economic facts*

## Industry

Oil-refining is the most important industry; Singapore has one of the largest oil-refining complexes in the world. The crude oil comes chiefly fom the Middle East.

Second place is taken by shipbuilding and repair. Singapore's shipyards produce not only ships but drilling platforms.

Then follow, in terms of output, the electrical and electronic industries (especially entertainment electronics, computer and communication systems), machine and vehicle manufacture, production of optical, scientific and medical instruments, chemicals, foodstuffs, rubber, textiles and building materials. Research and development are becoming increasingly important especially in the field of bio-technology.

## Trade

Only slightly less important than its diverse industrial production for the Singapore economy is trade (Singapore has one of the largest harbours in the world), especially foreign trade, which far exceeds the gross national product in volume. A considerable share is transit trade with neighbouring Malaysia (export of rubber, iron ore, zinc, copra and coconut oil).

Singapore is the gateway to world markets for the countries of the economic community ASEAN (Association of South-East Asian Nations), a loose association similar to the Economic Union (EU) whose members as well as Singapore and Malaysia include Thailand, Indonesia, Brunei and the Philippines.

The main trading partners are the USA (most important purchaser), Japan (most important supplier), Malaysia, the member states of the EU and Taiwan (Republic of China).

*Trading partners*

Singapore is heavily engaged in creating the "ASEAN Free Trade Area" (AFTA) modelled on the Common European Market. One of the suggestions in this direction made by the ASEAN states was rejected by the majority of the APEC states (Asean-Pacific Economic Cooperation) in 1991 but is planned for further discussion. There is, however, unity over the plan to dismantle the customs barriers in South-East Asia within the next 15 years.

## Tourism

Tourism has been an important source of income for the island republic for some time. Singapore may not be the first choice of holiday

## Economy

*Keppel Harbour, Singapore's international seaport*

destination but is popular for a relaxing stopover with long-distance travellers. It is likened to the "Switzerland of Asia" thanks to its good communications (important international airport; long-distance railway link with Malaysia and Thailand), wide selection of hotels and guest houses, and shopping facilities which cater for all the tourist's requirements.

**Number of visitors**

The immigration authorities registered almost 6 million visitors in 1992. Most visitors come from ASEAN countries, followed by the Japanese, Australians, Indians, US Americans and British.

**Length of stay**

The average stay of the 6 million visitors annually is about 3.7 days. The Singapore Tourist Promotion Board is trying to present the city's attractions more actively so as to increase the time people stay.

**"Singapore Cruise Center"**

Singapore is a popular port of call for cruise liners. 50 million S-$ were spent building the ultra-modern "Singapore Cruise Center" in the west of the city which can accommodate ships up to 245m/803ft long. Numerous shops, boutiques, banks, restaurants and hotels of a world-class standard greet the visitor – and there is even a small maritime museum.

**Tourist Infrastructure**

As part of the general prevailing drive for rapid economic expansion the city state is striving to expand its range and capacity in the service sector and has launched several projects to promote tourism. Sentosa Island with its wide range of attractions (e.g. a Grand Prix race track for Formula I and various new marinas) is the best example of this. These amenities are also popular with the indigenous population.

At the beginning of the Nineties Chinatown underwent extensive renovation which meant that some old buildings had to give way to modern ones.

**Future prospects**

One of the biggest projects for the future is the planned renovation of Singapore River and the buildings on the opposite bank. It is hoped to avoid the area being solely for tourists. In an effort to make the area north of Singapore River more attractive parks, pedestrian areas and other sights (culture and art centres, sculpture gardens and much more) are to be created.

## Agriculture, Fisheries

Agriculture is of limited importance in the modern industrialised city state of Singapore. Its share of the gross national product is below 1% and it only partly provides for Singapore's needs. At present about 3250ha/1315 acres of land are in agricultural use (in 1983 it was 6500ha/2630 acres) and that is for private livestock rearing (mainly poultry and pigs) and vegetables. In the long term the state has established so-called agrotechnological parks to stimulate agricultural production.

Agriculture

In recent years the growing of flowers (especially orchids), decorative plants and mushrooms has expanded.

The 1100 local professional fishermen are only allowed to fish in their own relatively small fishing zone. The resultant low catches can only meet a fraction of Singapore's demand for fish which by Asian standards is exceptionally high; the major share has to be imported from neighbouring countries.

Fishing

## Employment policy

The shortage of workers is a major problem for the economy of Singapore. For many years unemployment has been constant at 3%. Well educated workers and employees are poached so frequently by other companies that "job-hopping" has become a serious problem. This results in wages constantly rising.

Foreign workers are being recruited by the city state in ever-increasing numbers, at present there are about 250,000. Companies are advertising not only in Malaysia, China and India but also in the states of the former Soviet Union for qualified employees or even those willing to learn.

## Transport

Keppel Harbour, Singapore's harbour lies in a natural inlet on the south coast of the island. After Rotterdam it is the largest international seaport in the world and the principal centre of trade between Europe and the Far East. The modern docks can accept the largest sea-going ships, particularly the supertankers which deliver to the massive oil-refining complex.

Port

International container traffic makes up a significant share of the harbour's total trade (in 1992 about 190 million tonnes, 90 million tonnes of which were crude oil). There are huge docks which have modern repair facilities.

Keppel Harbour is the home port of the national shipping line "Neptune Orient Lines" (NOL). The merchant fleet sailing under the Singapore flag (including numerous ships sailing under other flags) lies in 12th position in the world with about 8 million BRT.

Changi International Airport is one of the most important centres of air traffic in South-East Asia. Situated at the eastern end of the main island it replaces the earlier airport Paya Lebar which was unable to cope with the rapid increase in volume.

Air travel

Equipped with every conceivable facility Singapore Changi Airport (also called "Airtropolis" on account of its futuristic architecture) is

**Transport**

*"Skytrain" at Changi Airport*

ready for the expected increase in traffic in the 21st century and ranks among the most modern airports in the world. Annually it handles about 117,000 flights operated by 57 airlines carrying 17 million pasengers. Following further expansion it should be able to handle up to 50 million passengers annually. Both terminals are linked by an ultra-modern "Skytrain".

Changi Airport has two runways for take-off and landing and is linked to the city of Singapore by a four-lane motorway. Video walls, changing art exhibitions, green areas, flower gardens and waterfalls are proof that Changi is more than just an airport. In Terminal 1 there is a swimming pool which overlooks the runway. Of course there are restaurants, discothèques, souvenir shops and duty-free shops.

Charter flights are handled at Seletar Airport in the north-east of the main island.

The national airline "Singapore Airlines" (SIA) is one of the largest air transport companies in the world, with the most modern aircraft flying to over 50 cities worldwide.

"Silk Air" the second national airline flies mainly to regional destinations.

Roads

The main island and city state are served by a relatively dense road network, part of which runs below the ground. At the same time the government is pursuing a policy of high costs for motorists which should dramatically reduce individual traffic. High taxes and immigration duties together with registration fees should make owning a car a luxury in the future. For road and rail traffic the Johore Causeway is the only link with the mainland. A second link with the mainland is planned to the west of Singapore (near the Malayan town of Kukup).

Rail

The Malayan railways operate as far as Singapore (terminus) which does not have its own railway network. The journey from Bangkok (Thailand) to Singapore (or in the other direction) is scenically very beautiful and takes about two days.

## Transport

In September 1993 a luxurious raillink was opened between Bangkok (Thailand) and Singapore. The "Eastern & Oriental Express" operates twice weekly and stops at the Malayan capital Kuala Lumpur (see Practical Information, Getting to Singapore).

Alongside a large fleet of taxis, buses and "trishaws" (tricycle + rickshaw, which only operate in the city centre now) the MRT (Mass Rapid Transport System), which came into operation at the end of 1987 and is now completed, caters for public transport.

Public transport

A cableway runs between Mount Faber and Sentosa Island. A bridge was built between the mainland and the island in 1992 near the World Trade Centre.

# Famous People

The following alphabetical list includes people who through birth, influence or death are connected with Singapore or Malaysia and have achieved international recognition.

**Aw Brothers**
(d. 1954 and 1956)
philanthropists
and patrons

Aw Boon Haw, the "Tiger", and Aw Boon Par, the "Leopard" were two celebrated millionaires and philanthropists who made their name as generous patrons of Chinese culture in Singapore, having made their money from medicinal mixtures based on Chinese herbal medicine. Their best known product was Tiger Balm, which proved effective for a variety of complaints.

In the Tiger Balm Gardens (see A–Z) they left a gigantic monument, with a profusion of colourful sculpture depicting scenes from Chinese mythology and traditional life as well as from modern Singapore (another "Tiger Balm Garden", named after the brothers can be found in Hong Kong).

**Joseph Conrad**
(Józef Teodor
Konrad
Korzeniowski;
3. 12. 1857 to
3. 8. 1924)
Polish writer

Joseph, born Józef Teodor Konrad Korzeniowski, was left an orphan and grew up in Russia in the care of relatives; then he went to the School of Seamanship in Marseilles and served in the French and later the British Merchant Navy. He acquired British nationality in 1884, gained his Master's Certificate and sailed the seas of South America and the Far East until 1894. Conrad, who learned English late but wrote his novels and stories in that language, was a masterly delineator of British seafaring life. He lived for several years in Singapore during the second half of the 19th c., gathering material for his novels of life in the East. Singapore and the life of Europeans in the city provided themes of works such as "Lord Jim", "The End of the Tether" and "The Rescue".

Other works by Conrad were "An Outcast of the Islands" (1896), "The Nigger of the Narcissus" (1897), "Heart of Darkness" (1902), "The Secret Agent" (1907) and "The Rover" (1923).

**Dr. Datuk Seri
Mahathir bin
Mohamad**
(b. 20. 12. 1925)
Prime Minister
of Malaysia
(from 1981)

The Prime Minister of Malaysia, Datuk Seri Mahathir Mohamad, was born in Alor Star in Malaysia. After attending school and training to be a doctor he became head of a private clinic but soon made a career in the National Organisation (UMNO), which was the decisive political power in Malaya (later called Malaysia) after 1945. He was Member of Parliament from 1964–69 but then left. In 1974 he was re-elected, took over the post of Education Minister and four years later Minister of Trade and Industry. In 1981 he became chairmen of UMNO and succeeded Premier Datuk Hussein bin Onn to become the new head of government in Malaysia. Dr Mahathir won elections in 1982, 1986 and 1990 with Malaysia experiencing the largest growth in the economy during his period of office.

**Goh Chok Tong**
(b. 1943)
Prime Minister
of Singapore
(from 1990)

When the "father of Singapore", Lee Kuan Yew (see entry) announced in June 1990 that he intended to step down from office in November 1990 it was clear that he would elect as his successor no other than his political "foster-son" Goh Chok Tong. In his acceptance speech Tong made it clear that despite a certain readiness to co-operate with the

*Sir Thomas Stamford Raffles, founder of present-day Singapore* ▶

## Famous People

opposition, which was growing in strength, he would only deviate slightly from the course of his predecessor. The main task of the government, according to this pragmatic politician, was the motto "Keep Singapore Strong!"

Goh Chok Tong was born in 1943 and took up politics on leaving school and completing his studies. In 1983 he became Defence Minister, two years later he was already deputy Prime Minister under Lee Kuan Yew.

**Lee Kuan Yew**
(b. 16. 9. 1923)
Prime Minister
of Singapore
1959–90

Lee Kuan Yew, was Prime Minister of Singapore for 31 years, when in government he was a pragmatic statesman whose policy was orientated towards the West and who was concerned to create out of the multi-racial population of Singapore a nation of Singaporeans.

Born in Singapore, the son and grandson of wealthy shipowners, he passed out of Raffles College in 1939 and took a law degree at Cambridge in 1946. Thereafter he set up in practice as a lawyer in Singapore (1950). Of his education he once said: "They wanted me to become an educated man, like an Englishman – the very picture of perfection! Like Nehru, I could weep when I think I speak English better than my mother tongue". He began his political career as adviser to various trade unions (1952), went on to found the left-wing People's Action Party (PAP, 1954) and finally (1959) became Prime Minister of the self-governing state of Singapore. Then, against the will of the Communist opposition, he played a part in the creation of the Federation of Malaysia (1963). Racial differences led in 1965 to Singapore's expulsion from the Federation, and on August 9th in that year Lee Kuan Yew declared the independent Republic of Singapore. In 1968, 1972 and 1976 his party, the PAP, won all the seats in the Parliament of Singapore although he led a strict regime. Even after his resignation in 1990 and stepping down in favour of his successor Goh Chok Tong (see entry) he is still known as his "grey eminence" – which is to say that no important decision is made without his approval.

**William Somerset Maugham**
(25. 1. 1874 to
16. 12. 1965)
British writer

The novelist Somerset Maugham ranks as the best European interpreter of the Malay character.

Born in Paris, Maugham studied medicine in Heidelberg and London but never practised as a doctor. He lived in London, New York and Paris and also spent several years in Singapore and Malaya, where some of his best short stories were written. When living in Singapore he stayed in the Raffles Hotel. His last years were spent on the Côte d'Azur, where he died in 1965.

His principal works were "Of Human Bondage" (1915), "The Moon and Sixpence" (1919), "The Circle" (1921), "The Painted Veil" (1925), "The Razor's Edge" (1944) and "Creatures of Circumstance" (1947).

**Sir Thomas Stamford Raffles**
(1781–1826)
"Founder of Singapore"

On the evening of January 28th 1819 Sir Thomas Stamford Raffles, Commercial Agent of the British East Indian Company, arrived at the mouth of the Singapore River in the course of a quest for a suitable site for a trading station, and on February 6th he acquired the island of Singapore from the Sultan Hussein Mohammed on behalf of the company. Within a few years he had destroyed the hitherto uncontested commercial monopoly of the Dutch, who had colonised the Indonesian island of Java. Raffles introduced Western conceptions of law and democracy into Singapore and founded the University.

Named after Sir Thomas Stamford Raffles are eight species with about 50 varieties of the parasitic plant called (*Rafflesiaceae*) which is related to rose bushes and has no chlorophyll. One of the best known species is *Rafflesia* which is widespread throughout South-East Asia and of which there are ten kinds; one, the Giant Rafflesia, is threatened with extinction. The plant has a diameter of up to one metre and can weigh up to 6kg.

## Famous People

H. N. Ridley, Director of the Singapore Botanic Gardens founded in 1859, planted the first rubber tree in Malaya in 1877, grown from seed smuggled out of Brazil. Despite the heavy resistance from the local farmers he succeeded in establishing the rubber tree and convincing the population of its economic value. By the turn of the century rubber production in Singapore and Malaya had overtaken that of South America and today Malaysia is still the largest producer of natural rubber in the world.

H. N. Ridley
(1855–1956)
Director of
the Botanical
Gardens of
Singapore

# History

|  |  |
|---|---|
|  | Since the history of Singapore is inseparable from that of the neighbouring Malay peninsula (now Malaysia) and since visitors to Singapore can make excursions into Malaysia (see A to Z section), this chronology takes in the development of Malaya as well as Singapore down to the time they became separate states. |
| 7th–14th c. | Seamen of the Hindu Kingdom of Srivijaya, coming from Sumatra and Java (Indonesia), settle on the Malay Archipelago. Prince Sang Nila Utama founds the kingdom of Temasek ("city on the sea"). According to the legend, he changes its name to Singa Pura ("lion city") after the appearance to him of a lion-like sea creature. |
| 1377 | The Malay Kingdom of the Majapahit Dynasty, based in Java, conquers the Malay Peninsula and destroys Singapore, which thereafter declines into a small and insignificant fishing village. |
| 1398 | Malays from Sumatra create the port of Malacca; a foundation which marks the beginning of the modern history of Malaysia and Singapore. Within a short time Malacca develops into the leading city in South-East Asia. |
| 1511 | The Portuguese navigator Afonso de Albuquerque takes Malacca. |
| 1606 | The Dutch East India Company allies itself with the King of Johore against Malacca. |
| 1641 | Malacca passes into Dutch hands. |
| 1786 | Britain takes a lease of the island of Penang. |
| 1795 | Britain takes over the Dutch colony of Malacca, but returns it to Holland in 1818. |
| 1811 | Singapore is annexed to the Malay sultanate of Johore and becomes the residence of Prince Temenggong. The population consists of a few hundred fishermen. |
| February 6th 1819 | Sir Thomas Stamford Raffles, agent of the British East India Company, arrives in Singapore and recognises the importance of its natural harbour for the expansion of British trade. He signs a treaty with Prince Temenggong Abdul Rahman for the establishment of a trading station. |
| 1824 | The population of Singapore has grown to 10,000, mainly through the immigration of Chinese coolies. |
| 1822 | Sultan Hussein Mohammed Shah cedes the whole of Singapore island to Britain in return for an annual payment of 5000 Spanish dollars. Britain also acquires Malacca from the Dutch in exchange for territory on Sumatra. |
| 1867 | Singapore becomes the seat of British administration on the Malacca Strait, subject (along with Penang and Malacca) to the Governor of Bengal. |
| 1874 | Although the British colonial authorities had begun to build up the new commercial settlement, the great wave of immigration from South China begins in 1874, with annual quotas of several tens of thousands. |

**History**

*The Padang at the turn of the century*

| | |
|---|---|
| Rubber tree seeds smuggled out of Brazil are planted by H. N. Ridley, Director of the Botanic Gardens. With John Dunlop's invention of the pneumatic tyre the rubber tree conquers the Malay peninsula. Singapore becomes a centre of the trade in natural rubber. | 1877 |
| Establishment of the first federation of the Malay sultanate under British protection. | 1895 |
| The sultanate of Johore accepts British protection. | 1915 |
| The Japanese General Tomoyaki Yamashita takes the island of Singapore (February 15th); capitulation of British forces under General A. E. Percival. The Japanese occupation is followed by a bloody massacre of the Chinese population. | 1942 |
| After the Japanese capitulation at the end of the Second World War Singapore returns to British hands (September 5th). Singapore and Malaya under British military government. | 1945 |
| Young Singapore intellectuals, graduates of British universities, strive for independence from British colonial rule. Singapore becomes a separate Crown Colony within the new Federation of Malaya. The first election of a legislative assembly is held on March 20th; a majority of the members are appointed by the British colonial authorities. | 1948 |
| The Communist Party of Malaya seeks to establish a government in Malaya and Singapore by force of arms. The Communist cadres had gained in strength during the jungle war, in which they had fought alongside British forces. The British declare a state of emergency. It takes 12 years to quell Communist guerilla activities. | 1948–60 |

# History

*Singapore about 1907*

| | |
|---|---|
| November 21st 1954 | The 31-year-old lawyer Lee Kuan Yew, a Cambridge graduate, founds the People's Action Party (PAP), which aims at full sovereignty for Singapore, in association with an independent Malaysia. Singapore is granted full internal self-government. |
| August 31st 1957 | Malaya becomes an independent and sovereign member of the Commonwealth. |
| June 3rd 1959 | After Singapore's first free elections Lee Kuan Yew becomes its first Prime Minister. |
| September 16th 1963 | Foundation of the Federation of Malaysia, with Singapore as a member. |
| 1965 | Singapore leaves the Federation of Malaysia. The independent republic of Singapore is founded and becomes a member of Commonwealth and United Nations (UN) (August 9th). Lee Kuan Yew becomes the first Prime Minister. |
| August 8th 1967 | The south-eastern countries of Singapore, Thailand, Malaysia, Indonesia and the Philippines form the Association of South-East Asian Nations (ASEAN). The Association developed as a reaction to the growing threat of Communism in Indochina. It is primarily an economic community modelled on the European Union but is increasingly becoming a political alliance providing mutual military assistance. |
| 1971 | Dr Benjamin Sheares (non-party) becomes President (d. 1981). |
| 1981 | The former Indian trade union leader and co-founder of the Republic, Devan Nair, becomes the new President following the death of Benjamin Henry Sheare. |

## History

| | |
|---|---|
| The socialist People's Action Party (PAP) led by the Prime Minister Lee Kuan Yew wins the elections again. Although they only have 13% of the votes only two seats are lost owing to the electoral laws based on the British first-past-the-post system. Both the opposition parties win a seat, the Workers' Party and the Singapore Democrat Party.<br>   Brunei becomes a member of ASEAN. | 1984 |
| On September 2nd the Chinese Wee Kim Wee becomes Singapore's new President, succeeding Devan Nair. | 1985 |
| The Port of Singapore is the fourth largest for exports in the world after Amsterdam (Holland), Kobe (Japan) and New Orleans (USA). | 1986 |
| The new Changi Airport is opened, one of the most modern in the world.<br>   The first routes of the urban railway (MRT) come into operation. | 1987 |
| Lee Kuan Yew is voted in for a further four years. With 64.4% of the votes the People's Action Party (PAP) win 80 of the 81 seats. The elections took place early owing to growing internal opposition but only resulted in one seat being gained because of the first-past-the-post system. | 1988 |
| Parliament confirms President Wee Kim Wee to another four years in office. | August 31st 1989 |
| Lee Kuan Yew resigns and names his successor Goh Chok Tong (49). | June 1990 |
| The change of leader takes place but Lee Kuan Yew remains "spiritus rector" of the government. | November 1990 |
| New elections take place and the PAP gain 77 of the 81 seats. Chok Tong's popularity falls and only 61% of the electorate vote for him. Three seats go to the "Singapore Democratic Party" and one to the "Workers Party". The governing party automatically wins 41 seats as the opposition cannot oppose all the seats. | August 31st 1991 |
| In Seoul (South Korea) the third conference of APEC takes place (Asian-Pacific Economic Cooperation). The suggestion by the six ASEAN countries to form an economic community in East Asia modelled on the common market within the European Union (Asean Free Trade Area, AFTA) is rejected, but the conference participants agree to dismantle customs barriers in South-East Asia within the next 15 years. | November 1991 |
| At the 26th ASEAN conference in Singapore it is decided to establish a forum which should include twelve other countries (including China, Russia, Vietnam, Laos, Papua New Guinea) as well as the six ASEAN countries. ASEAN itself, founded in 1967 as a bulwark against the threat of Communism, will try to reach a dialogue with its former Communist neighbours (unofficially also with the Peoples' Republic of China). "Preventative diplomacy" is intended to create political stability in this economically fastest-growing region in the world. | July 1993 |
| As expected the victor in the first democratically held presidential elections is the former vice-prime minister and leader of PAP, Ong Teng Cheong (57). The only opponent was the 67-year-old banker and administrator Chua Kim Yeow; two candidates from the People's Workers' Party were not allowed to stand. The election was necessary because President Wee Kim Wee, who, like his three predecessors, had been appointed as a purely ceremonial head of state in 1985 and had | August 29th 1993 |

**History**

announced his retirement from active politics on September 1st 1993 at the age of 77.

Cheong, like his opponent a member of PAP, will, following a constitutional change, have more far-reaching powers than his predecessor Wee Kim Wee. The new president can apply his veto against cabinet decisions, in household affairs and in other government business.

# Singapore in Quotations

Wee came to the entraunce of the straights of Sincapura.... We wentt 4 or 5 leagues, all the way on both hands soe full of creekes, passages and Ilands, as I never saw the like, especially on the starboard side, the little Iles lying like soe many Haicocks laid close together all overgrowne with trees
*Travels in Europe and Asia*, 1637

Peter Mundy
(17th c.)

Singapore, a vision of green hills and red dust, a sickly odour of pepper, cocoa, nut-oil and drains.
*From Pekin to Calais by Land*, 1889

Harry de Windt
(19th c.)

People in Singapur are dead-white – as white as Naaman – and the veins on the backs of their hands are painted in indigo.
   It is as though the Rains were just over, and none of the womenfolk had been allowed to go to the hills. Yet no one talks about the unhealthiness of Singapur. A man lives well and happily until he begins to feel unwell. Then he feel worse because the climate allows him no chance of pulling himself together – and then he dies.
*From Sea to Sea*, 1889

Rudyard Kipling
(1865–1936)

Singapore, the capital of the Straits Settlements at lat. 1° 17' north, long. 103° 51' east on the island of the same name off the south coast of the Malayan peninsula, owing to its location at the entrance to the China Sea, one of the most important centres of world sea traffic and of great strategic importance, therefore heavily fortified, was founded in 1819 on the site of a Malayan settlement by Sir Stamford Raffles and together with the island ceded to the British government by the Sultan of Johore. Its name Sinhapur means Lion City in old Indian. As a free port, in contrast to the Dutch contract policy, it quickly developed into the main centre of trade in South-East Asia and prospered with the opening of the Suez Canal. The population numbered 10,000 in 1822, 40,00 in 1840, 162,000 in 1891 and 228,550 in 1911, among them 3825 Europeans and Americans, 4120 Eurasians, 164,040 Chinese, 38,080 Malayans and other people native to the archipelago, 17,825 Annamites, Siamese, Burmese, Japanese, etc. The garrison has 2050 men and consists of a batallion of local infantry, two British companies and a local artillery regiment and half a company of pioneers comprising a volunteer corps made up mainly of Eurasians.

Baedeker's
"India" (1914)

I hear that a year or two back there was a mutiny in Singapore of which we heard practically nothing. A local native regiment got loose and started murdering people, rushing up and down the streets asking everybody if he was English. Those who said "Yes" had their throats cut at once. One English wag said that he was Irish. They let him, and the others who followed his example, alone. Presently one of His Majesty's ships came round the corner, and I understand that the bluejackets did their work very thoroughly indeed . . .
   The mutineers seemed to have special aversion to golfers, who were surprised to find themselves being murdered in the bunkers.
*My Journey Round the World*, 1921.

Alfred Viscount
Northcliffe
(1865–1922)

The Van Dorth Hotel in Singapore was everything but luxurious. The bedrooms were shabby and the mosquito nets patched and darned; the bathrooms, all in a row and separate from the bedrooms, were gloomy and musty. But it had character. The people who stayed here, masters of travel, whose journey ended here in Singapore, mining

Somerset
Maugham
(1874–1965)

engineers without work and planters who were here on holiday, created in my opinion a far more romantic atmosphere than the elegant folk, world travellers, government officials and their wives, well-to-do businessmen, who gave lunch in "Europe", played golf, danced and were altogether proper."

Singapore is a meeting point of many races. The Malays, although the sons of the soil, live restlessly in towns and are only few; and it is the Chinese, moving, watchful and hard-working who populate the streets; the dark-skinned Tamils tread softly barefooted, as though they were just passing visitors in a strange land, but the Bengalese, groomed and prosperous feel at home in their surroundings and are self-confident; the Japanese, cunning and obsequious, appear to be busy with urgent and secret business; and the English with their topees and white linen suits racing past in cars or at a leisurely pace in rickshaws, have a casual and carefree appearance.
*"The Four Dutchmen"*, 1922

Noel Barber

(The City of Lions)
That was his first impression of Singapore, and although Raffles was always more interested in what the future held than how things were at present, we still know what the island had once looked like, from a report compiled by Captain Ross – a marine expert with the John Company: he raised Singapore to the status of "town" in his writings:

The town of Singapore, on the island of the same name, lies on the tip of land near the western part of a bay (it is easily recognisable from the welcoming hill which is partly without trees and lies directly behind the town); between the town itself and the west end of the bay there is a channel where local ships lay anchor off the town; this could also prove useful for lighter European vessels to load up.

On the east side of the bay – opposite the town – there is a deep inlet lined with mangrove trees, which would also make a good anchorage for local boats; and roughly north of the low, sandy part of the bay there is a village inhabited by busy fishermen; a short way eastwards a path through the mangroves leads to a freshwater river.

(The last years of peace)
From 1869 onwards, when the Suez canal was opened – two years after Singapore became a Crown Colony –, the era of steamers brought unlimited prosperity for the island, which in fact (to once again use the hackneyed expression) lay at the crossroads of the Orient. In the first three years after Lesseps opened the canal the tonnage of ships using the port of Singapore jumped from 200,000 to 700,000 t. Soon afterwards there were three-mile-long wharves in Tanjong Pagr.

When Kipling came to Singapore for the first time he saw "a good five miles of ships' masts and chimneys in the harbour area". He also saw the streets, blocked with traffic: a select mixture of steam trains, ox-carts, horse-drawn carts and the first rickshaws to have come from Shanghai to Singapore. It was chaos. . . .

(Today and Tomorrow)
Just like Hong Kong Singapore was and is faced with the problem of land shortage. Every centimetre counts. And so the housing problem could only be solved by building upwards. By 1980 three-quarters of the island's population will be living in tower blocks built by the government. Of course, living in high buildings inevitably causes problems such as vandalism and suicide; not only because of the soullessness of these flats (their effect on the occupants is unpredictable), but because of the opportunity they offer to commit suicide. The majority of suicide victims in Singapore end their lives by jumping off high-rise blocks of flats.
*"The Singapore Story"* From Raffles to Lee Kuan Yew

**Singapore in Quotations**

TRISHAW                                     Tung Hung
On the busy streets of Singapore
There slowly paddled the old-fashioned trishaw
Slowly paddled trishaw
Carries its own sorrow

On the back lane parks the trishaw
On the back lane near the food-stall —
Two bowls of porridge and a plate of salted vegetables —
The trishaw-rider is having his meal — thirty cents in all

Slowly paddled trishaw, with no customers at all
The rich have their cars after all
The young ones take their buses —
The trishaw has no customers at all —

The trishaw has no customers at all
The only few it has —
The haggard cabaret girls and stingy old women
Who bargain to the single cent.

Slowly paddled trishaw, with no customers at all
With no customers at all
Yet it paddled so slow
'cause it carries too much its own sorrow

# Singapore from A to Z

The following alphabetically arranged entries appear under their English titles as is common practice in Singapore.

**Note**

MRT = Mass Rapid Transport System

Suggestions for planning a short visit to Singapore can be found under Sightseeing Programme in the Practical Information Section.

## Abdul Gaffoor Mosque

See Little India

## Alkaff Mansion

F 1

The Alkaff Mansion is one of four mansions belonging to the prosperous Arab Alkaff family. Up until Sheik Abdul Rahman Alkaff bought it following his arrival in Singapore (about 1850) it was called Mount Washington.

Extensive renovations have changed it into an exclusive restaurant with a floor area of 780sq.m/8393sq.ft and from the terrace there is a magnificent view over the southern part of Singapore.

The building itself combines several architectural styles, the dominant influences being Dutch, British and Arabian with some Asian set pieces. Before it is a large flight of steps.

Alkaff Mansion is surrounded by a wonderful tropical garden, entry is only permitted when dining in the restaurant (pre-booking advisable; tel. 2 78 69 79). It is renowned for Indonesian "rijstafel", an Indonesian-Dutch speciality.

**Address**
10 Telok Blangah Green

**Opening times**
daily 10am–midnight

## Arab Street

B/C 4/5

Arab Street runs between Canal Road and Beach Road. This is the shopping centre of the Islamic population of Singapore – the Malays, Arabs, Pakistanis and Muslim Indians. It is a street of little shops in which the buyers and sellers haggle over the price. Here visitors will find not only gaudy Asian fabrics but also traditional gold and silver jewellery. The goldsmiths will make pieces to order, to any desired design and at prices which are often surprisingly reasonable. There are also bespoke tailors offering a 24-hour service.

Arab Street is most conveniently reached from Beach Road. At the intersection with North Bridge Road is the Sultan Mosque (see Sultan Mosque).

**Bus**
13

**MRT**
Bugis

## Armenian Church

C 4

The Armenian Church (Armenian Apostolic Church of St Gregory the Illuminator), completed in 1835 by Armenian refugees from Turkey, is Singapore's oldest Christian church. It was designed by the architect George D.

**Location**
Hill Street

◀ *The lavishly sculptured façade of the Sri Mariamman Temple*

# Bird Park

*The Armenian Apostolic Church, Singapore's oldest Christian church*

**Bus**
124, 173, 174

**MRT**
City Hall

Coleman, its name commemorates the first cleric of Singapore's Armenian community.

It is no longer used for worship but is protected as a national monument. It stands at the foot of the oldest Christian cemetery in Singapore laid out in 1822, on Fort Canning Rise, also known as the Forbidden Hill (see Fort Canning Park).

The Armenians were once one of the most powerful economic groups in Singapore; they owned, among other things, the Raffles Hotel (see entry). Today only about 60 still live here.

In the same street is the Chinese Chamber of Commerce (see entry).

Armenian Street

Also of interest is the old Tao Nan School in adjoining Armenian Street, a typical product of the turn of the century architecture.

## Bird Park

See Jurong Town

## ★Botanic Gardens                                             B 1

**Location**
Cluny Road/
Holland Road

**Bus**
7, 106, 174

**Opening times**
Daily
5am–midnight

**Admission free**

The Botanic Gardens, laid out by the British authorities in 1859 for research purposes, are among the most beautiful tropical gardens in the world, with more than half a million plants. A pavilion in Victorian style houses the largest herbarium in Asia. The gardens used to be outside the actual city centre but today they are only a short distance from Orchard Street and form part of the almost continuous green belt which runs through Singapore giving it the character of a garden city.

In 1877 the British Director of the Botanic Gardens, H. N. Ridley, planted the first rubber trees in Malaysia here on an experimental basis. The experi-

**Bugis Street**

*The Botanic Gardens – one of the most beautiful tropical gardens in the world*

ment was successful, and by the turn of the century natural rubber had become the most important commercial product of Singapore and Malaysia.

These gardens, which are among the most beautiful tropical gardens in the world, cover an area of 52ha/130 acres. Four hectares are devoted to an "unspoilt jungle area" with huge trees, lianas as thick as a man's arm, giant ferns and a profusion of tropical flowers, which give an authentic picture of Singapore's original natural vegetation. Many species of animals also live in the gardens.

| | |
|---|---|
| Equally impressive is the Orchid Pavilion with more than 2500 plants from 250 different species, in which the various stages in the development of orchids, from seeds to blossom, are displayed in glass vessels. Among them is the national flower of Singapore, the orchid *Vanda Miss Joaquim*. | Orchid Pavilion |
| A beautiful lake decked with water-lilies and inhabited by black swans adds to the charm of the Botanic Gardens. | Lake |
| A good two hours should be allowed for visiting the gardens, but half a day or more could easily be spent there. | Note |

## Bugis Street    C 4

The history of Bugis Street is perhaps typical of the city of Singapore and its attempts to present the visitor with a "clinically clean city in the tropics". The new Bugis Street has hardly anything in common with its historic forerunner, once the hotbed of "the most beautiful transvestites in Asia". Even the original location had to make way for a station in 1985. The new Bugis Street retains little of the original character despite the reconstruction costing 6.8 million US $. The attempts by the city fathers to recreate

**Location**
Albert Street

**MRT**
Bugis

some of the former atmosphere are visible, apart from some architectural pieces from the old Bugis Street, small restaurants and foodstalls have reappeared, but the overall atmosphere is one of boredom. It is only worth making a detour here to shop at the night market which is open until 4am.

The Buginese, former inhabitants of this quarter, came from Celebes and Borneo (Indonesia), where they lived on the coasts and were feared as pirates. Their culture is similar to that of the Malays and Javanese and is influenced by Islam. Nowadays the Buginese have been assimilated into Singapore's way of life.

## Bukit Timah Nature Reserve          off map

**Location**
Bukit Timah Road
12km/7 miles
north-west

**Bus**
171, 173, 182

Bukit Timah is the largest of Singapore's nature reserves, with an area of 81ha/202 acres, and also the most unspoilt (cars prohibited). Here well-maintained footpaths with rest huts at intervals, run through primeval jungle. The tigers which formerly inhabited Singapore's forests are no longer to be found, but there are still large families of monkeys.

"Bukit" is Malay for "mountain" – Bukit Timah is the highest point in Singapore.

## Butterfly Park

See Sentosa Island

## Central Beach

See Sentosa Island

## Central Park

See Fort Canning Park

## ★Changi Airport          off map

**Location**
east of the
city centre

**Bus**
390, 97, 125, 131

The airport at Singapore, Changi Airport, is (at least until the new airport at Hong Kong is completed) the largest centre for air traffic in South-East Asia. It has been described by experts as "the world's most attractive airport".

Opened in 1982 and completed in 1987 Changi Airport is one of superlatives: in 1992 it handled 17 million passengers and has yet to reach its capacity planned for the 21st century. Even so extensive expansion is being planned with capacity for up to 50 million passengers.

Changi Airport, also called "Airtropolis", is a small town in itself with a complete infrastructure. Several hundred thousands of people are occupied in providing the incoming or departing passengers with everything that Singapore hospitality can offer.

Up to 350 aircraft a day land on and take off from the two parallel runways, both 4000m/13,123ft long and 60m/197ft wide. From Singapore there are flights to 100 cities in over 50 countries with 57 airline companies having offices at Changi Airport.

# Changi Beach

*Tomorrow's architecture: Changi Airport*

The airport administration is proud of the speedy turnround of passengers. Up to 48 jumbo jets can be handled simultaneously and even then it should only take twelve minutes from the passenger leaving the aircraft to collecting his luggage from the console. The journey to the centre of Singapore 20km/12 miles away does not take much longer on the four-lane city highway.

Both passenger terminals contain every conceivable comfort. Apart from shops and boutiques, duty-free shops and banks there are restaurants, bars, discothèques and other entertainment amenities. A wide screen cinema, for which there is no charge, makes waiting for the flight more enjoyable. A swimming pool with a sun terrace overlooking the runways is being built in Terminal 1.

The Singapore Tourist Promotion Board has even thought of passengers who are just changing flights at Changi Airport. Those landing before 2 or 4pm and whose connecting flights are later than 6 or 8pm can take part in a free two-hour tour of the city without having to undergo official entry procedures. The tours depart daily at 2.30 and 4.30pm from in front of Terminal 2.

*Free tours of the city*

## Changi Beach     off map

This beautiful beach on the eastern tip of the island, not far from Changi Airport, is part of an eight hectare park area and planted with cinnamon trees and sea almonds. Unfortunately the rural character of the Upper Changi Road has been lost with modern urban development.

**Location**
Upper Changi Road

The sandy beach leads west to the Changi Sailing Club in Serangoon Harbour with excellent water sport facilities. Scuba enthusiasts should contact the Singapore Sub-Aqua Club, tel. 4 45 62 53.

**Chesed-el Synagogue**

*Evening on Changi Beach*

## ★Prisoners Chapel

**Opening times**
Mon.–Fri.
9.30am–noon
and 2–4.45pm
Sat.
8.30am–12.30pm

**Admission free**

A visit to the small museum at the former Changi prison is a sobering experience. It commemorates the horrors perpetuated by the Japanese during the Second World War and the occupation of Singapore.

An impressive collection of photographs by the Australian George Aspinall documents life in the prison camp. Nearby is the Prisoners Chapel where prisoners' names are immortalised by their regimental inscriptions.

## ★Chesed-el Synagogue    C 3

**Location**
Oxley Rise

**MRT**
Somerset

This Jewish synagogue was established by Sir Reuben Manasseh Meyer, a Jew of German origin, in 1905, which explains why it is sometimes also called after him. It is regarded as one of the masterpieces by the colonial architects Swan & Maclaren. The synagogue is still used by the small Jewish community in Singapore and is maintained by the founder's descendants.

## ★★Chettiars Hindu Temple    C 3

**Location**
Tank Road

**Bus**
123, 143, 195, 198

The original Chettiar Temple, dedicated to the Hindu god Subranium (also known as Muruga or Sri Dhandayuthapam), the Preserver, was built in 1855. It was built by the South Indian caste, the Chettiars, who traditionally follow the trade of money-changers. The temple is among the richest in Singapore and one of the greatest Hindu temples in South-East Asia.

*The ornate Rajagopuram, Chettiar Temple* ▶

**Chinatown**

It underwent rebuilding several times, finally being demolished in 1979 and replaced by a larger more impressive new building designed in the original style.

The ornate sculptured decor – especially the 23m/75ft-high Rajagopuram, the tower above the entrance door – was carried out by masters from the renowned Mamallapuram Sculpture School in Madras. It houses 48 stained glass windows also produced in India. The Shive shrine in the courtyard conceals a rarity, a Thoonganai maadam, representing the rear end of a resting elephant. Even in India, the home of Hinduism there are only four such sacred objects.

**Thaipusam**

The temple is noted for the macabre Thaipusam festival (see Practical Information, Events), a Hindu festival of penance and thanksgiving celebrated at the beginning of January or the beginning of February (varying according to the lunar calendar). The worshippers carry, in honour of Subramaniam, a minature temple known as the kavadi which may weigh anything up to half a hundredweight. While in a trance they pierce their cheeks and tongue with spikes and spears up to three metres/ten feet long.

**Navarathiri**

In October the temple is the scene of a more joyous celebration, the festival of Navarathiri or the Nine Nights (see Practical Information, Events), which is accompanied by classical dances and traditional music; on the 10th day a silver horse is paraded through the streets.

## ★★Chinatown                                                        D/E 3/4

**Location**
South Bridge Road/
New Bridge Road
Area

Since Singapore was founded in 1819 it has been mainly refugees from the provinces of southern China who have settled here. Within an area of more than two square kilometres 75,000 people lived in houses closely packed together in narrow lanes and alleys. Singapore's Chinatown is a carry-over

*Chinatown of old . . .*                              *. . . and of today*

# Chinatown

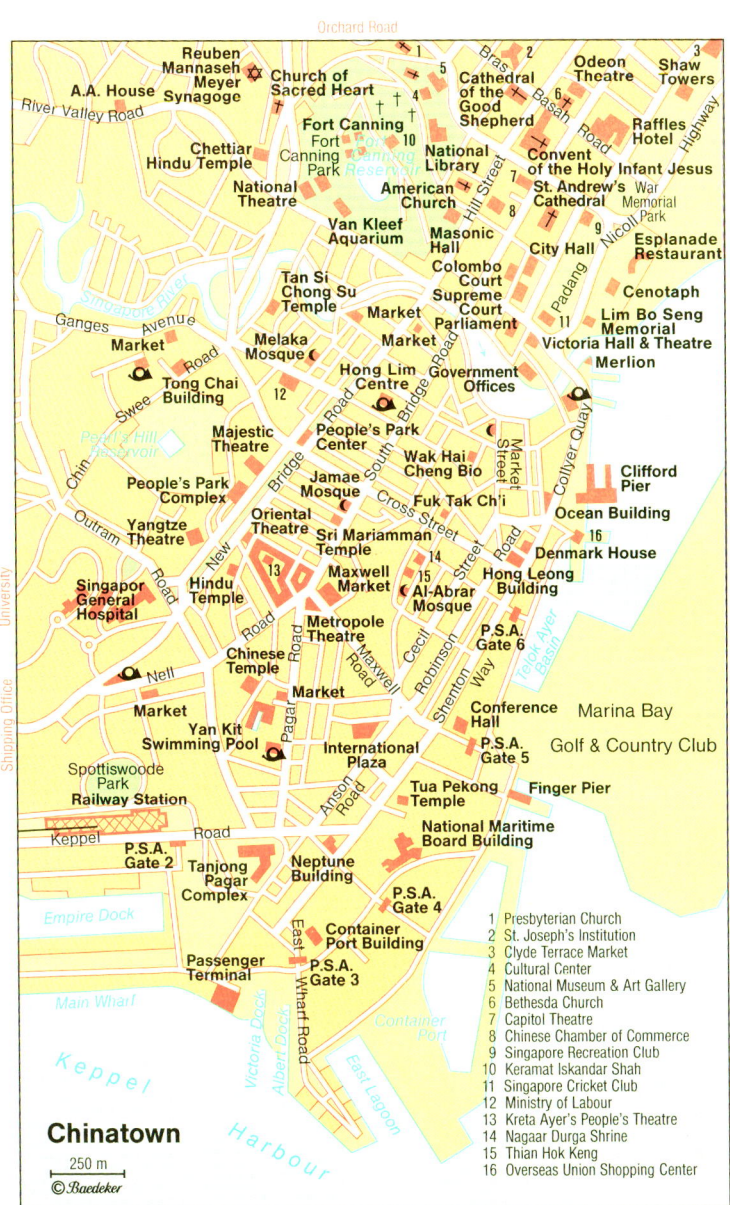

1. Presbyterian Church
2. St. Joseph's Institution
3. Clyde Terrace Market
4. Cultural Center
5. National Museum & Art Gallery
6. Bethesda Church
7. Capitol Theatre
8. Chinese Chamber of Commerce
9. Singapore Recreation Club
10. Keramat Iskandar Shah
11. Singapore Cricket Club
12. Ministry of Labour
13. Kreta Ayer's People's Theatre
14. Nagaar Durga Shrine
15. Thian Hok Keng
16. Overseas Union Shopping Center

## Chinese Chamber of Commerce

**Bus**
124, 143, 174, 179

**MRT**
Outram Park

from the time when a three-storey building anywhere in the town was regarded as a skyscraper.

Architecturally it is a mixture of traditional Chinese building and the British colonial style, to which Chinatown owes its colonnades. Later, well-to-do Chinese visiting Europe brought back classical features with them. The resultant style congomerate is known as Chinese Baroque. Chinatown ends at the Singapore River (see entry), where, on the opposite bank, the modern world begins.

History

Sir Thomas Stamford Raffles personally gave instructions for the layout of a town which was "to reflect the varied interests of all races and classes". He had areas laid out for the Bugis, the Malay, the Arabs, the Chulias and the Chinese – thus Chinatown came into being. Up until the present day it has stood in contrast to the so-called European town on the other side of the Singapore River. It is the expression of a self-contained culture in which the traditional way of life has been preserved. When it became a conservation area in 1986 Chinatown was threatened with massive rebuilding programmes which would have certainly destroyed its character. Perhaps that is why one still comes across Chinese soothsayers, although their trade is prohibited in Singapore.

The "death houses", however, had to give way to civic development. Any Chinese resident of Singapore who did not have enough room to die with the traditional pomp and ceremony of a traditional Chinese funeral, could, until a short time ago, hire one of the "death houses" in Sago Lane.

Present day appearance

Several roads have since been restored, the old Tanjong Pagar Road is particularly impressive. However, restoration is restricted to the fabric of the buildings. Traditional little workshops have given way to modern shops so that Singapore's Chinatown has lost much of original atmosphere. There is little of the street life left which was nurtured by the Chinese immigrants.

The various aspects of Chinese Baroque may have been preserved – in Trengganu Street, Pagoda Street, Temple Street, Club Street with its many branches, or Boat Quay – but the old traditions are slowly dying. This is especially true of the rhythm of life and old crafts in Chinatown. The candlemakers are to be found in China Street alongside small noodle factories. In Peking Street joss sticks are made. The figures of gods for Chinese temples are carved in Club Street. The tailors of Chinatown will make shirts, suits and other items of clothing at a day's notice.

Future outlook

How long will Chinatown continue to exist? The traditional inhabitants of Chinatown cannot afford the rents in the restored buildings; new tenants and owners are moving in who only use the façade of Chinatown but do not bring back its soul. It is to be feared that this Chinese quarter which was once so famous and steeped in tradition will one day become a mere tourist attraction.

Street markets

The once-famous street markets of Chinatown as well as the street kitchens have been moved to the newly built Kreta Ayer Complex in Sago Lane, a concrete silo without any style. Here both the morning markets and the Pasar Malam night market (see Markets) are held.

Street kitchens

For the benefit of the more apprehensive visitor it should be said that the food served in the street kitchens will not disagree with a Western stomach. The authorities are very strict about hygiene.

# Chinese Chamber of Commerce C 4

**Location**
Hill Street

The Chinese Chamber of Commerce occupies a tall modern building which incorporates traditional Chinese architectural elements.

**Crocodile Farm**

Note, in particular, the pagoda-style double curving roof, the very fine mosaics on the surrounding walls, modelled on those in the Imperial Palace in Peking, and the richly ornamented red main doorway in traditional Chinese palace style.

Although the government of Singapore kept (official) contact with the People's Republic of China to a minumum in the past, the Chinese presence is now becoming more apparent in the city state. At the 26th meeting of ASEAN in July 1993 China was not involved in a forum for economic and political co-operation, however, it is certain that it is in the interest of the Singapore government to nurture contact behind the scenes.

**Bus**
124, 173, 174

**MRT**
City Hall

## Chinese Garden

See Jurong Town

## ★Clarke Quay                                                    D 4

Not far from the estuary of the Singapore River into the South China Sea four streets have recently been turned into attractive pedestrian zones lined with 80 old gas lamps and planted with trees. Five old buildings of historical significance have been carefully restored and now house 176 shops and 17 night spots (restaurants, pubs, bars with live music and discothèques). There is also a fruit and vegetable market and some street kitchens. On the bank of the Singapore River four old barges (tongkangs) are moored and have been converted to floating restaurants. The total area of 21,000 sq.m/226,674sq.ft invites the visitor to wander about and at night time it is quite lively. A boat ride through Clarke Quay Adventure with its own special effects promises excitement. The planners of Clarke Quay have estimated for up to 18,000 visitors daily.

Clarke Quay is named after Sir Andrew Clarke, the second governor of Singapore. Some of the restored buildings commemorate traders and merchants from the days of old Singapore.

**Location**
Singapore River

**MRT**
Raffles Place

## Clifford Pier

See Keppel harbour

## Coralarium

See Sentosa Island

## Crocodile Farm                                                  off map

Hundreds of crocodiles, alligators, lizards and snakes are bred for Singapore's leather-working industry. Feeding times provide an exciting show for visitors. Most of the skins, after tanning and polishing, are sold to leather-working firms, but some of them are used on the farm in the manufacture of souvenirs (Singapore being renowned for its high quality crocodile skin products) for sale to visitors.

Souvenirs purchased should be accompanied by a certificate stating that the product originates from a breeding farm as crocodiles are protected by the "Washington Biodiversity Agreement".

**Location**
Upper Serangoon Road

**Bus**
111, 118

**Opening times**
daily 9am–5pm

**Crocodile Paradise**

*Crocodiles – raw material for the leatherwork industry*

## Crocodile Paradise

See Jurong Town

## Cuppage Road Market

See Markets

## East Coast Park Lagoon                                                                             off map

**Location**
East Coast Parkway

**Bus**
16

**Opening times**
Mon.–Sat.
9am–6.30pm,
Sun. 8am–6.30pm

It is not even a quarter of a century since this present day leisure park of Singaporeans, East Coast Park Lagoon, was covered by water. The land was reclaimed to create a recreational area for the population where they can picnic, swim, sail and surf, cycle, play golf and squash or fly kites.

This artificial lagoon must be the largest swimming pool in the world: it is the equivalent of forty Olympic-size indoor pools. One half of the lagoon is reserved for swimmers the other for beginners at wind surfing.

The lagoon is supplied with water by the South China Sea but the waves are machine-made. "Big Splash" the swimming area can accommodate 6000 bathers and has 17m/56ft high chutes down which bathers can hurtle into the swirling waters of the pool. Changing rooms are, of course, available.

At the East Coast Sailing Centre there is windsurfing on the lagoon or out on the open sea. Beginners can take an introductory course of two three hour sessions and hire boards. Tennis courts are available (tel. 4 49 51 18). The East Coast Recreation Centre has 17 squash courts for hire (tel. 4 49 05 41). On the nearby Parkland Driving Range (tel. 4 40 67 26/3 48 56 09) there is a golf practice range with 48 driving ranges.

**Fish Markets**

Alongside picnic facilities and street kitchens hungry guests can visit the Lagoon Food Centre north of the lagoon with food and drink typical of Singapore, its kitchens specialising in the preparation of seafood.

Close by is the Bicycle Hire Centre where bicycles can be hired on an hourly basis to explore the park.

## Elizabeth Walk

See Queen Elizabeth Walk

## Emerald Hill                                                                                   B/C 3

The Emerald Hill district, and in particular the old buildings in the area, are protected as national monuments. Here, as in Chinatown (see entry), the predominant style is Chinese Baroque, a mingling of traditional Chinese elements and the British colonial style. Later this colourful architecture was still further enriched with features taken from European Renaissance and Baroque, producing an architectural style found only in Chinese colonial territories.

The lower part of Emerald Hill, which joins with Orchard Road, is also called Peranakan Place. The Peranakan were the ethnic mix of early Chinese immigrants with the native Malays, the women were referred to as "Nonya" and the men as "Baba". These so-called Straits-born Chinese have a different culture from the Chinese immigrant community. This can be seen in Peranakan Place and is reflected in the original cuisine of the street restaurant with a beer garden.

The small Peranakan Museum documents this period. A typical Peranakan house has been faithfully reconstructed.

**Location**
Emerald Hill Road/Orchard Road

**Bus**
7, 13, 14, 16, 23, 64, 65, 92, 105, 106, 111, 118, 123, 124, 132, 139, 143, 167, 171, 173, CBD 1

**MRT**
Somerset

**Opening times**
daily 11am–6pm

Peranakan Museum

## Empress Place                                                                                  D 4

This landscaped park was laid out in 1972 on a site which had previously been a car park. Here, after the last war, the statue of Sir Stamford Raffles, founder of modern Singapore, which had been pulled down by the Japanese, was re-erected.

Named after the British Queen Victoria, the Empress Place lies below the Victoria Memorial Hall (see entry) and the Victoria Theatre.

At the Empress Place on the east bank of the Singapore River, a copy of the Raffles Statue marks the spot where he is said to have landed in 1819.

On the marble base are inscriptions in the four principal languages of Singapore (Malay, Chinese, Tamil and English) recording the foundation of the town.

The Empress Place Building on the Singapore River with its impressive Georgian style of architecture was built in 1865 and was once part of the courthouse. Today it is a museum of Chinese culture with valuable exhibits on loan from the People's Republic of China.

**Location**
North Boat Quay

**Bus** 850

**MRT** City Hall

Raffles Statue

Empress Place Building

## Fish Markets

See Markets

**Fort Canning Park**

*In the Empress Place Park*

## ★Fort Canning Park (Central Park)     C/D 3/4

**Location**
Clemenceau Avenue

**Bus**
123, 139, 143, 164, 180, 195, 204

**MRT**
Dhoby Ghaut

**Opening times**
daily 5am–11pm

This large park of some 40ha/100 acres, situated in the middle of the city of Singapore, sometimes referred to by its old name Central Park, is both a place to relax and a meeting place for the people of Singapore. It contains the Old Christian Cemetery, laid out in 1822 but with only a few graves being maintained, the National Theatre, the National Museum (see entry), the Van Kleef Aquarium (see entry), the Cultural Centre and closeby is the River Valley Swimming Pool.

The main attraction is a large floral clock. The walks around Fort Canning Hill offer fine views of the Victoria Memorial Hall, the dome of Singapore's Supreme Court and the Singapore River (see entries) with the old warehouses and ultra-modern office buildings. All that remains of the former British Fort Canning is a heavy gate dating from 1846.

Forbidden Hill

Fort Canning Rise was formerly known as Bukit Larangan, the Forbidden Hill. According to tradition Sultan Iskander Shah, last Malay ruler of Singapore, was buried on the hill after the destruction of his kingdom in 1391 by the Majapahites (a Sumatran ruling family). His tomb is venerated by the Muslim Malays as a keramat, holy place. This was the site of ancient Singapura. Recent excavations have brought to light gold instruments and pottery of an early Malay settlement. The finds, which caused a great sensation, are exhibited in the National Museum (see entry).
   The Sultan Mosque (see entry) was built by the Sultan Iskander Shah.

## Fort Siloso

See Sentosa Island

*The Hajjah Fatima Mosque (See page 56)*

## Fuk Tak Ch'i Temple       E 4

The Fuk Tak Ch'i Temple (Temple of Prosperity and Virtues) is one of the oldest Chinese temples in Singapore and is accordingly ornately decorated.

Built in 1825 it is the religious shrine of the Shenists, a sect which combines the thoughts of Confucius, mythical Chinese popular beliefs, and Buddhism.

The illustration inside the left-hand gate is noteworthy: it represents the god of riches dressed in mourning.

Gamblers hoping for advice on how to win are regular visitors to the Fuk Tak Ch'i Temple.

**Location**
Telok Ayer Street

**Bus**
CBD 1

**MRT**
Raffles Place

## ★Geylang Sera       off map

Geylang, a distortion of the Malay kelang (factory) serai (lemon grass), is one of the oldest Malay areas of Singapore. Good examples of colonial architecture and Chinese Baroque can be seen.

There are big celebrations held here at Hari Raya Puasa (see Practical Information, Events).

**Location**
Geylang Road

**Bus** 7

**MRT**
Aljunied

**Hajjah Fatima Mosque**

## ★ Hajjah Fatima Mosque                                                B 5

**Location**
Java Road

**Bus** 13

**MRT**
Bugis

Built in 1845 this is the oldest Islamic mosque in Singapore. This charming little mosque was built by a Malay Lady Hajjah Fatima in token of her love for a nobleman of the Bugis community. Hajjah Fatima, her daughter and son-in-law are buried behind the mosque.

Many elements of European classicism can be seen in its design, for example, the Doric pilasters on the minaret, handiwork of the French architectural company Brossard Mopin, who restored the mosque in 1932.

## ★★ Haw Par Villa (Tiger Balm Gardens)                          off map

**Location**
Pasir Panjang Road
8km/5 miles west
of Singapore

**Bus**
10, 30, 51, 143

**MRT**
Buono Vista
then SBS bus 200

**Opening times**
daily 9am–6pm

**Admission fee**

This Confucian Madame Tussaud's or Disneyland is an immense and colourful advertising display, devoted to glorifying the product after which the gardens are named, on a lavish scale such as could only be found in Asia.

The many acres of the gardens are filled with gaudy representations, in plaster, concrete and papier mâché, of scenes from Chinese mythology, outsize jungle animals, a plump and jolly Buddha, American, Greek and Italian themes, scenes from Chinese country life and the life of Singapore's streets, often with a moralising or didactic slant.

One theme which is constantly emphasised, however, is the virtues of Tiger Balm, recommended for every conceivable purpose.

The Tiger Balm Gardens were established after the Second World War by the brothers Aw Boon Haw and Aw Boon Par (see Introduction, Famous People) who had made millions from the sale of Tiger Balm – still a very popular household remedy which proves effective against a variety of aches and pains.

*In the Tiger Balm Gardens, the "Confucian Madame Tussaud's"*

*In a Singapore temple*

The Aw brothers also devoted part of their fortune to various good causes, including the provision of free coffins for the poor, and presented their valuable collection of jade to the state (see National Museum).

The Haw Par Villa has been recently restored. It houses several theatres, including a puppet theatre, in which several cultural events are held every day. For information on ticket reservations tel. 7 74 03 00.

**Note**

## High Street

D 4

With more than 40 large stores and several hundred smaller shops, the High Street is one of Singapore's busiest shopping streets. Here are offered for sale optical and electronic appliances made by the world's best known manufacturers and watches and jewellery by the world's most celebrated designers. There are numerous bespoke tailors whose fabrics range from Chinese silk to Irish linen (see Practical Information, Tailormade Clothing). Some of the best shops for jade, pearls and traditional jewellery are to be found here.

**Bus**
124, 173, 174

**MRT**
City Hall;
Raffles Place

**Opening times**
daily 10am–10pm

## ★Hong San See Temple

C 3

The forerunner of this Chinese temple was built in 1829 by Chinese immigrants from the province of Fukien in nearby Tras Street. The temple is consecrated to the master of benefactors, Kok Seng Wang. It was demolished when the city was expanded and rebuilt in its present form in 1908. Today it is one of the city's protected national monuments.

Based on the design of Chinese palaces with numerous courtyards it successfully combines elements from pagan, Taoist, Buddhist and Con-

**Location**
Mohamed Sultan Road

**Bus**
16, 65, 92

House of Tan Yeok Nee

**MRT**
Somerset

fucian schools of architecture. This is no doubt the reason it is frequented by worshippers from several different faiths.

The wood carving, frieze and interior sculptured decor are of interest.

## House of Tan Yeok Nee                                                                 C 3

**Address**
Clemenceau Avenue/
Penang Road

**MRT**
Dhoby Ghaut

The House of Tan Yeok Nee dates from 1885 and was built in the style typical of rich merchants. Tan Yeok Nee, who came from southern China, started out as a simple tailor but worked up to become a wealthy businessman. Much of the building material (tiles, granite, etc.) was imported from China resulting in a house typical of south China.

Nowadays the House of Tan Yeok Nee is the Singapore headquarters of the Salvation Army.

## Insectarium

See Sentosa Island

## Japanese Garden

See Jurong Town

## ★★Johor Bahru                                                                     Malaysia

**Location**
about 25km/
15 miles north

**Bus**
Singapore–Johor Express (Bansan Street Terminus)
Bus 170 (Queen Street and Bukit Timah Road) departs every 10 mins.

Johor Bahru is capital of the Malaysian sultanate of Johore, the seat of government and royal residence of the Sultan of Johore. It lies on the north side of Johore Strait (Selat Johor) on the Malaysian mainland, linked with Singapore by the 1038m/¾ mile long Causeway.

The sultanate of Johore which takes in the south of the Malacca peninsula is one of 13 states of the constitutional monarchy of Malaysia. The area was first developed in the mid-19th c. by the Chinese who planted pepper. At the beginning of the 20th c. rubber plantations were introduced. Johore produces the largest quantity of pineapples in Malaysia.

The town (founded by Sultan Abu Bakar in 1855) and surrounding area contain many relics and reminiscences of Malaysian history. Visitors contemplating a trip to Johor Bahru can obtain information from the Malaysian Tourist Development Corporation (see Practical Information, Information).

## Abu Bakar Mosque

**Location**
Jalan Abu Bakar

**Opening times**
Outside times of prayer

This royal mosque, built in 1892 by Sultan Abu Bakar, stands on Jalan Aby Bakar, a street running parallel to the Johore Strait. Its architecture shows a mingling of the Moorish with the British colonial style. The combination is remarkably successful, making this one of the finest Mosques in Malaysia.

Visitors are admitted outside the hours of prayer.

# Johor Bahru

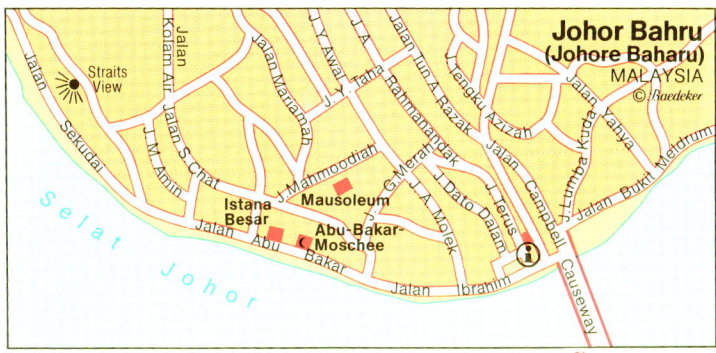

## Istana Besar

The ceremonial palace of the Sultan of Johore, the Istana Besar, also situated on the Jalan Abu Bakar, was built in 1866 as the first residence of the royal family. The palace is now used only for official functions (receptions, coronations and various royal ceremonies); the Sultan lives in a new palace, the Istana Bukit Serene, which is not open to the public.

Like the Abu Bakar Mosque, the Istana Besar is built in a style which mingles Moorish and British colonial features, and is decorated with traditional Malaysian carving. In the north wing is the throne room, and adjoining this a small museum displaying Court dress, the royal insignia, weapons and hunting trophies.

The palace can be seen with a permit from the Johore tourist authorities (Jalan Wong Ah Fook, Johor Bahru, tel. 22 35 91).

**Location**
Jalan Abu Bakar

**Opening times**
Palace: Mon.–Sat.
9am–noon (with permit);
Garden: daily
all day

## Istana Garden

The 53ha/21acre palace gardens, which are open to the public throughout the day, are among the most beautiful in Malaysia. Particularly fine are the orchid garden and the fern garden. There is also a Japanese garden with a Japanese tea-house, created in honour of a visit by the Crown Prince of Japan in 1936 and a small zoo with indigenous animals.

## Kota Tinggi

See entry

## Kukup

This typical Malaysian fishing village lies north-west of Johore Bahru on the Malacca straits.

Romantically situated its restaurants are renowned for their excellent fish dishes.

**Location**
40km/25 miles
north of
Johore Bahru

## Royal Mausoleum

This has been the burial place of the royal family of Johore since the foundation of the town.

The Mausoleum itself, in a style modelled on Arab architecture, is not open to the public, but there are many other interesting Muslim tombs in the cemetery.

**Location**
Jalan Mahmoodiah

## ★Jurong Town off map

**Bus**
From Jurong Interchange
250, 251, 253

**MRT**
Jurong

Jurong is Singapore's most modern industrial zone, almost an independent town.

Here, in a garden-like setting on land reclaimed from swamp, some 2400 firms have established themselves, including some specialising in high quality micro-electronics. However, the petro-chemicals industry is a predominant element and Jurong has one of the largest refineries in the world.

In Jurong there are also extensive parks. Most interesting are the Chinese and Japanese Gardens as well as the Bird Park.

## Chinese Garden & Japanese Garden

**Opening times**
Mon.–Sat.
9am–7pm
Sun., pub. hols.
8.30am–7pm

**Admission fee**

**Bus**
From Jurong Interchange
242, 406

**MRT**
Chinese Garden

The Chinese Garden of Jurong covers an area of over 13ha/32 acres, with a network of footpaths providing easy access to its beauties. Entered by an imposing gateway, the garden contains several pagodas, a stone boat, a nine-arched bridge and a Chinese tea-house.

The architecture, in a style modelled on that of the Sung Dynasty (960–1279), is reminiscent of the Summer Palace in Peking.

The Chinese Garden is a favourite background setting for wedding photographs. On Saturdays newly married couples can be seen smiling into the photographer's camera: in front of a pagoda, in the "Moon Inviting Boat" or on the White Rainbow Bridge.

The Seiwaen Japanese Garden covers over 13ha/32 acres of typical Japanese garden layout with stone gardens, goldfish ponds, Lotus ponds, stone lanterns and little pagodas.

## Bird Park

**Bus**
From Jurong Interchange
250, 251, 253

**MRT**
Jurong

**Opening times**
Mon.–Sat.
9am–6pm,
Sun. and pub.
hols. 8am–6pm

**Admission free**

**Bird tour**
daily 10.30am

Jurong Bird Park, established in 1971, occupies an area of 20ha/50 acres on the hill of Bukit Peropok in the centre of the town, and is one of the largest parks of its kind in the world. Over 1000 birds from all over the world are housed in 24 aviaries and include flamingoes, birds of paradise, emus, ostriches and rare tropical birds. A 2ha/5 acre "flight garden", 20m/66ft high, in which the birds live in surroundings resembling their natural habitat, allows them to be studied at close quarters. There are bird shows daily at 10am, 10.45am, 3pm and 4pm and organised photograph sessions twice daily (11.30am and 3.30pm).

Visitors are free to walk around the park or they can take a trip round it on a miniature railway. A third alternative is the monorail opened in 1991. The route runs past an artificial waterfall which plunges over a granite crag 30m/100ft high into an artificial river which flows through the park.

The ponds, lakes and lagoons are the haunt of every species of waterfowl, and there is even a penguin pool – the park's most popular attraction – in which, with the help of supplies of ice, the penguins, not otherwise found in the tropics, are made to feel at home. Feeding times are a popular attraction (daily 10.30am and 3.30pm).

Breakfast with the birds

Between 9am and 11am daily the visitor can have breakfast with the birds.

**Jurong Town**

## Jurong Crocodile Paradise

As well as being a breeding centre for crocodiles the Jurong Crocodile Paradise is also a tourist attraction surrounded by extensive gardens. It has an underwater viewing gallery, a dark cave, a giant goldfish pond, a stage where shows are held and two restaurants.

Crocodile Paradise is home to about 3000 crocodiles which are involved in a variety of performances: "Jumping Crocodiles" can be seen any time, feeding times are Monday to Friday at 10.15am and 5pm.

Crocodile leather is also on sale.

**Location**
Jalan Ahmad Ibrahim

**Bus**
251, 253, 255

**MRT**
Jurong East

## Singapore Science Centre

This excellent display of hands-on exhibitions provides a modern and attractive introduction to the sciences. The children's section is particularly well thought out. The visitor has the opportunity to carry out certain experiments for himself.

The main emphasis is on physics, natural history, chemistry, space travel and computer science. It also has a planetarium, temporary exhibitions and a restaurant.

A major attraction is the Omni Theatre with its three-dimensional screen. Action-packed films about science and space travel give the spectator the impression of actually being in the middle of the scene.

Apart from Mondays there are performances daily between 3pm and 8pm, Sundays from 2pm.

**Bus** 143, 158

**MRT**
Jurong East

**Opening times**
10am–6pm
(closed Monday)

**Admission fee**

Omni Theatre

*Keppel Harbour in the early morning (See page 62)*

Kelongs

## Kelongs  off map

**Location**
Southern Islands

**Bus**
To Ponggol: 64, 65, 106, 111 to Serangoon Road, 83, 84
To Tuas: 174 to Jurong Crescent, change to 175

The kelongs of Singapore are a traditional type of fish-trap, used by the Malays for many hundreds of years. Long bamboo poles are driven into the sea bottom at points where it is relatively shallow, and on these is constructed a platform bearing a small hut. Some of the larger kelongs are like miniature villages.

The kelongs are to be found around the offshore islands but are no longer included in the excursion programme organised by the Singapore Tourist Board, although information is available from them. Anyone interested in a visit to a kelong should seek the help of the proprietor of one of the seafood restaurants in Ponggol or Tuas, which are usually supplied by the kelongs.

## Keppel Harbour F/G 1–3

**Bus**
TIBS 850

**Boats**
Clifford Pier

**MRT**
Raffles Place

Keppel Harbour is the world's second largest international seaport after Rotterdam. It occupies a natural inlet at the southernmost point of Singapore and is the base of the national shipping line "Neptune Orient Lines" (NOL).

It can accept up to 600 vessels at the same time, and in 1991 handled over 190 million tonnes of freight, about 90 million tonnes of which were crude oil (see Facts and Figures, Transport).

Clifford Pier is the oldest part of the port installations but is no longer the main dock for overseas ships since the opening of the new "Cruise Center" near to the World Trade Center in western Singapore.

Keppel Harbour is still an interesting sight at any time of day, with its tankers and freighters, together with hundreds of Chinese junks, barges and sampans operating as lighters.

Tours of the harbour

Clifford Pier is also the departure point for harbour and island cruises. The harbour cruise goes round the various wharves and also takes in the container port, whereas the island cruise visit Malay fishing villages and some of the 54 islands lying off the main island of Singapore. Information and reservations from the Terminal Building, first floor.

See also Practical Information, Boat Cruises and Information.

## ★Keramat Habib Noh F 3

**Location**
Palmer Road

**Bus** 167

**MRT**
Marina Bay

In this most important of Malay-Muslim shrines in Singapore, built in the style of a mausoleum, Habib Noh bin Mohammed al-Habshi is buried.

The Malay Muslims believed that this holy man of the last century possessed supernatural powers which made him invisible.

## ★Kong Meng San Phor Kark See Temple  off map

**Location**
Bright Hill Drive

**Bus** 132

**MRT**
Ang Mo Kio

This temple was only built in 1981 yet it is the largest religious establishment in Singapore.

It comprises mainly Thai and Chinese architectural styles arranged according to the art of Chinese geomantics "feng shui" (see Facts and Figures: Religion, Superstitions). Close by is a large Chinese cemetery.

## Kota Tinggi                                                    Malaysia

Kota Tinggi is a small town in the sultanate of Johore. The road from Johor Bahru (see Johor Bahru), capital of the sultanate, passes by large pineapple plantations. Johore's pineapples, reputed to be the sweetest in the world, are grown for canning and export.

**Location**
On the road from Johor Bahru to Mersing (about 85km/53 miles north of Singapore)

Kota Tinggi's main sights are its falls and its recreational park. Kota Tinggi Falls, about 9km/6 miles east of the town, tumble from a height of 35m/115ft into a natural basin

The area around the falls has been developed as a recreation area, with picnic and bathing facilities. Overnight accommodation is available in a modest cottage hotel. The hill of Gunung Muntahak (624m/2047ft) offers scope for adventurous jungle walks.

Gunung Muntahak Park

Bus: See Practical Information, Bus Trips.

## Kranji War Memorial                                              off map

Round Kranji War Memorial are buried victims of the Second World War, 4000 men and women, representing the 20,000 who lost their lives in 1942 resisting the Japanese invasion and occupation. The memorial, a 25m/80ft high mast topped by a golden star, bears the inscription "They died for all free men" in six languages (Chinese, English, Malay, Tamil, Urdu and Gurkhali).
In a cemetery are graves honouring important personalities.

**Location**
Mandal Road/ Woodlands Road

**Bus**
182

*In the Kuan Yin Temple (See page 64)*

Kuan Yin Temple

## ★Kuan Yin Temple C 4

**Location**
Waterloo Street

**Bus**
7, 13, 14, 16, CBD 1

**MRT**
Bugis

This Taoist temple, dedicated to the goddess of mercy, is one of the most popular Chinese temples in Sinagapore. Here, appealing to the goddess Kuan Yin, the Chinese seek peace and protection from the adversities of life. The main hall houses three altars. The central one is dedicated to the goddess Kuan Yin, the two side altars to the sage Ta Ma tan Shith and a famous doctor of the Han Dynasty (3rd c.), Hua Tua, a patron of Chinese healing. At the back there is an altar to Buddha. The statue of the goddess in the main hall of the temple is clad in many layers of silk, votive offerings from grateful worshippers. The temple is the scene of busy ritual activity. The original Kuan Yin Temple dating from 1884 was demolished in 1982 and rebuilt retaining most of the original structure.

## Kusu Island off map

Location

Kusu is one of the 54 smaller islands which surround the main island of Singapore. It lies 7km/4½ miles south of the city. According to legend Kusu was once a turtle which turned into an island to save shipwrecked Chinese and Malays.

Boats: From World Trade Centre (ferry) Mon.–Sat. 10am–1.30pm, Sun., pub. hols. 9.45am–5pm at 1½ hourly intervals; return 1 hour after departure from W.T.C.

## Tua Pek Kong Temple

The principal feature of interest on the island is a Taoist temple dedicated to Tua Pek Kong, the Chinese god of fortune. The delicately curving pagoda

*Chinese Temple, Kusu Island*

*Beach on Kusu Island*

roofs are supported on columns, some of which stand on the rocky sea bottom. The best time to visit the temple is at the end of October and the beginning of November, when the Kusu Festival (see Practical Information, Events) is celebrated and large numbers of gaily decorated sampans moor at the temple. The festival lasts a month, and during this period the god shows himself liberal in granting prosperity to those who pay him respect.

On a hill in the middle of the island is a keramat, a Malay shrine, dedicated to Syed Abdul Rahman, a Malay noble, and his family, who mysteriously disappeared from here in the 19th c.

The ascent is lined with votive offerings, nowadays more symbolic in the form of rather ugly plastic bags. Both the temple and keramat are respected equally by the Chinese and Malays.

## *Little India

B 4

The Indian quarter of Singapore, known as Little India, is centred on Serangoon Road. A visitor to this part of the city, surrounded by men in dhotis (loincloths) and women in colourful saris, could be excused for believing himself suddenly transported to India. The shops in this quarter sell spices, herbs and other foodstuffs from India, Indian arts and crafts, silk and muslin, brocades and cotton. Small Hindu temples lie hidden in the side streets. The noise and chatter of the streets and markets are drowned by a mixture of classical dance and temple music, or hit tunes from Hindi films.

**Location**
Serangoon Road

**Bus**
64, 65, 92, 106, 111

**MRT**
Bugis

## Abdul Gaffoor Mosque

Also in the Indian quarter is the mosque commissioned by Sheik Abdul Gaffoor bin Sheik Hyder around 1909. It is a fine example of classical Indian Islamic architecture which successfully blends Saracen and Roman elements.

**Location**
Dunlop Street

MacRitchie Reservoir

# MacRitchie Reservoir                                                                                                                off map

**Location**
Lornie Road

**Bus**
104, 132, 167

**MRT**
Toa Payoh

The MacRitchie reservoir holds 315 million litres/70 million gallons of rainwater. The surrounding area has been laid out as a park, with many attractive footpaths.

Concerts are occasionally given in the pavilion above the reservoir, and there is a floating fountain which constantly changes its form and is illuminated after dark to produce an enchanting pattern of light and water.

## ★★ Malacca                                                                                                                            Malaysia

**Location**
about 250km/
150 miles
north of Singapore

Malacca, also called Melaka, lies about halfway between Singapore and Kuala Lumpur, the capital of Malaysia. It is well worth taking a two-day trip to this centre of Malaysian history if time permits, for Malacca makes a rewarding complement to a stay in Singapore.

**Note**

For information on getting to Malacca see Practical Information, Bus Trips and Information.

**Importance**

Malacca is the capital of the Malaysian state of the same name, one of four ruled by a Governor instead of a Sultan.

**History**

The town, situated at the mouth of the Malacca River, was founded by Sultan Iskandar Shah in the 13th c., and was the capital of the first Malay kingdom, which by about 1400 was exchanging Ambassadors with China. The king reigning at that time in Malacca was Parameswara, ruler of the Hindu-Malay kingdom, which had moved its capital from Singapore to Malacca. Parmeswara married a Chinese princess, and this alliance made the town, with its natural harbour, the commercial centre of South-East

Santiago Gate

Tranquera Mosque

Asia, dealing mainly in condiments and spices. Islam was brought to Malacca by Arab traders, and from there spread all over the Malay peninsula. In 1511 the Portuguese captured the town and the Malay ruler fled to Johore. The Portuguese admiral Albuquerque, encouraged mixed marriages between his troops and Malay girls, and the descendants of these unions still live in the Portuguese village of Malacca and speak a medieval form of Portuguese. In 1614 the town was taken by the Dutch, who 150 years later ceded it to Britain in exchange for British-held territories on Sumatra.

Malacca is a focal point of Malaysian history. The different periods of that history and the various rulers who have held sway here have left their mark in the form of historic old buildings, some of them still excellently preserved. Malacca's past is also reflected in a lively trade in antiques.

Malacca has now lost its importance as the commercial centre of South-East Asia, a role taken over by Singapore. Its harbour, of which a Portuguese seaman once wrote "Malacca is the richest seaport in the world, with the largest number of traders and of ships", is now largely silted up.

## A Famosa (fortifications)

Not much of the original solid and extensive fortifications of A Famosa, built around 1512 by the Portuguese Alfonso de Albuquerque, can be seen today. Yet it is still the symbol of the town of Malacca even though only the

Above the town

## Malacca

*Exterior of the Cheng Hoon Teng Temple, Malacca...*

gateway named Porta da Santiago at the foot of Regency Hill remains. This gate, which is a reconstruction from 1670, the original having been shot to pieces during the Dutch siege, was almost destroyed after the occupation of Malacca when the British set about razing to the ground all fortifications. It was only the veto of Sir Stamford Raffles that prevented it from being demolished. The coat of arms of the East Indian Trading Company can be seen on the gateway.

## Bukit China

**Location**
Jalan Bukit China

This hill on Jalan Bukit China, the street named after it, is occupied by the largest Chinese cemetery outside China. Some of the tombs date back to about 1400. Of the palace of the Chinese princess Hong Lim Poh, who became the wife of King Parameswara and lived here with 500 maids-in-waiting, there remain only a few foundations.

## Cheng Hoon Teng Temple

**Location**
Temple Street

This Taoist temple is the oldest and most lavishly decorated Chinese temple in Malaysia. Built in 1704 by a wealthy merchant named Chang Ki Lock, it is dedicated to the Chinese admiral Cheng Ho, Peking's special envoy at the Court of Malacca, who later achieved divine status.

Among its most striking features are the pagoda roofs, decorated with glazed filigree reliefs depicting scenes from Chinese myths. In the main hall is an altar with lacquer-painting of the utmost delicacy on the front. In the side halls are stelae representing the dead, which in Taoist belief are visited from time to time by the souls of the ancestors so that they may be supplied with food by their descendants.

... and the interior

## Chinatown

In this quarter around the Malacca River there are still many houses dating back more than 200 years, some of them ancestral family homes notable for their magnificence. They are the finest examples of the style known as Chinese Baroque, a mingling of Chinese features, colonial influences and classical-style borrowings from Europe.

In this area, too, particularly in Jonker Street, are Malacca's antique shops, tempting the buyer with furniture, domestic equipment, traditional jewellery and fine porcelain, through which a summary of the town's history can be seen.

**Location**
West of Town Square

## Christ Church

This Anglican church was originally built by the Dutch in 1753, using red bricks brought by sea from Holland. The walls were later given a facing of red laterite. Note in particular the roof beams, each sawn from a single log, and the old tombstones, with inscriptions redolent of Dutch history. The silver Communion vessels still bear the Dutch coat of arms.

**Location**
Jalan Laksamana

## Light and Sound Show

Every evening at 8pm (in Malay) and at 9.30pm (in English) a grandiose "Light and Sound Show" brings Malaysian history to life at the Jalan Kota: the arrival of the Malay people, their colonial suppression and their regained freedom.

**Location**
Jalan Kota/ Padang

**Admission fee**

# Malacca

*Chinese tombs in the Bukit China Cemetery, Malacca*

## St Paul's Church

**Location**
Jalan Kota

St Paul's Church is now a ruin, though the outer walls have been restored. The Church on Residency Hill, was founded in 1521 by the Portuguese Governor Albuquerque, and was the episcopal church of St Francis Xavier, Bishop of the Portuguese possessions. It passed into the hands of the Dutch in 1753.

There are a number of old tombstones in ruins.

## Stadthuys

**Location**
Jalan Laksamana

The old Town Hall, built in stages between 1641 and 1660, is probably the oldest Dutch building in South-East Asia. Its sturdy red-brick walls, massive wooden doors and window gratings have withstood the ravages of time.

The building is now occupied by Government offices. In an adjoining 300-year-old Dutch house is the Museum, with a variety of artefacts – few in number, but interesting – illustrating the history of Malacca.

## Tranquera Mosque

**Location**
Jalan Tranquera

**Opening times**
Outside times
of prayer

This 150-year-old mosque on the coast road to the north of Malacca is an unusual example of Islamic architecture in Malaysia. While most mosques follow Arab models, this one – a building of several storeys with a saddle-shaped pagoda roof – is modelled on the architecture of Sumatra (Indonesia). This style, developed by the Minangkabau ethnic group on Sumatra, was brought to Malacca by Sumatrans who conquered south-western Malaysia during the Malay migration towards the end of the first millennium A.D.

The interior of the mosque is very simple; the walls are faced with fine decorative tiles. There is a mausoleum said to contain the remains of Sultan Temenggong, who ceded Singapore to Stamford Raffles in 1819.

# Malaysia

See Johor Bahru, Kota Tinggi and Malacca

## ★Mandai Orchid Gardens

off map

The Mandai Orchid Gardens are the largest of their kind in Singapore, with an area of 4ha/10acres, and have the widest range of species. The finest orchids of South-East Asia are cultivated here and exported all over the world. Some of the plants grown here reach a height of up to 3m/10ft.

The gardens are situated on a hillside surrounded by primeval forest and contain beautiful man-made lakes with water lilies and other tropical plants.

Singapore is one of the main orchid exporters in the world; the 250 or so orchid farms export over 20 million orchids annually.

Owing to the proximity of the Mandai Orchid Gardens to the Zoological Gardens of Singapore (see Zoological Gardens) it is worth combining a visit to both places into one day.

**Location**
Mandai Lake Road

**Bus** 123, 171

**Opening times**
daily
8.30am–5.30pm

**Admission fee**

**Note**

## ★Marina Bay

D 4

This huge park, a kind of permanent garden show, was built on land reclaimed from the sea. There are numerous amusements and recreational facilities as well as some restaurants.

It is very popular with many Singaporean families at weekends.

**Location**
Marina South

**MRT**
Marina Bay

*The Mandai Orchid Gardens, orchid cultivation*

**Maritime Museum**

*Mandai: the largest collection of orchids in Singapore (See page 71)*

## Maritime Museum

See Sentosa Island

## ★ Markets

Singapore would not be a true Asian city without its markets. The idyllic street markets and street kitchens, however, have had to give way to modernisation and have been moved into sterile concrete blocks.

Chinatown

The happy chance, by which markets once spread over every empty spot in Chinatown, has been restrained by the new Kreta Ayer Complex in Sago Lane, in the very place where the death houses used to provide their service for the poor. The early morning market is open daily from six to ten and the night market, the Pasar Malam, from six to ten.

The hygienic setting, however, has not altered the exotic variety of merchandise. Here are sold various Chinese medicines, even the sight of which may sometimes be too much for a Western stomach (perhaps a decoction of seahorses in wine, seasoned with powdered rhinoceros horn as an aphrodisiac?). The snakes which can be seen squirming about in a cage are also destined for the cooking pot. The grasshoppers beside them serve both as delicacies for human consumption and for the nourishment of caged songbirds.

*A stall in one of Singapore's night markets* ▶

**Memorial Hall and Victoria Theatre**

| | |
|---|---|
| Fish Markets | There are many fish markets in Singapore, but the most picturesque is the one at Jurong, which has a daily turnover of 2000 tonnes. On account of the high turnover the market is strictly controlled. Visitors unconnected with the trade need an official permit and tourists are, therefore, recommended to visit the fish market at Ponggol, near the Hougang housing complex, which is open every day from 3am. Sharks, the fins of which are used to make the delicately flavoured shark's fin soup, are now a rarity. Lobsters and giant prawns, however, are common throughout South-East Asia. |
| Serangoon Market | This traditional market is now held in the Zhu Jiao Complex in Serangoon Road. There are sections for the Muslims, whose meat must be ritually slaughtered; here, too, there is a trading outpost of India, and of course, all the colour and variety of Chinese food which, from what we hear, includes everything from the water, the land and the air, except submarines, tanks and aeroplanes, since no one has yet devised a suitable marinade for them! The market is open in the morning and in the evening from 6–10pm. |
| Cuppage Road Market | This market, which handles merchandise from all over the world, has also been transferred to a permanent building. Perishable goods which will not keep fresh are sold in tins – great mountains of tins. Here, too, there are Chinese hot food stalls. |
| Night markets | The night market (Pasar Malam) is open daily from 6pm to 10pm. There is also a night market in the restored historic centre Singapore River. At Boat Quay between South Road and Elgin Bridge fruit, vegetables, handicrafts and antiques are on sale. |

## Memorial Hall and Victoria Theatre

See Victoria Memorial Hall and Victoria Theatre

## Merlion Park                                                                                             D 4

**Location**
On Singapore River

**Bus** 124, 173, 174

**MRT**
Raffles Place

At the outflow of the Singapore River into the Singapore Strait, in a small park, stands an 8m/26ft high figure of a merlion, the lion-like sea monster said to have appeared 700 years ago to Prince Sang Nila Utama, who gave Singapore its name. The merlion is now the emblem of the island republic.

From the park there are charming views of the harbour.

## Ming Village                                                                                          off map

**Location**
Pandan Road

**MRT**
Clementi, then
SBS bus 78 + 32

**Opening times**
daily 9am–5.30pm

The Ming Village is Singapore's only remaining pottery and the largest of its kind in the region. A wide variety of both hand-made and manufactured traditional porcelain from different Chinese epochs is produced. Among them are almost perfect copies of famous faïences from the Ming and Quing dynasties, for example, which only an expert could distinguish from the real thing.

For those who just want to look and not buy it is still possible to watch highly skilled craftsmen at work.

*The merlion, emblem of Singapore, in Merlion Park* ▶

**Mount Faber**

*Viewing platform, Mount Faber*

## ★Mount Faber                                                                                      F 1

**Location**
West of Singapore

Rising to a mere 120m/395ft above sea-level, Mount Faber can hardly be called a mountain; but it is high enough to afford fine views of the city of Singapore, some of the offshore islands and, in clear weather, of the Indonesian island of Sumatra. At night the city below the hill is transformed into a bluish unreality, a sea of lights, ocassionally traversed by the flashing navigation lights of jumbo jets approaching the airport. Those who find the evening air too cool for them can watch the spectacle from the comfort of a restaurant.

Cableway to Mount Faber

On Mount Faber is the mainland station of the cableway to Sentosa Island (see Sentosa Island).

## Musical Fountain

See Sentosa Island.

## Nagore Durgha Shrine                                                                              E 3

**Location**
Telok Ayer Street

**Bus** CBD 1

**Opening times**
daily 9am–5.30pm

The Nagore Durgha Shrine was built in 1829 by Muslims who settled in Singapore from South India. The mosque is also called the Masjid (= mosque) Chulia.

The façade flanked by two towers is of an interesting design, combining a striking mixture of Doric columns and Islamic or Indian elements. It is of symmetrical proportions with each floor of the upper part of this imposing building displaying a different style of window.

**National Stadium**

*View of Singapore from Mount Faber*

## National Museum                                                         C 4

The National Museum, built in neo-classical style, was founded in 1887. It is in three sections, all of which are of great interest – the Museum proper, the Art Gallery and the Haw Par Jade Collection.

The museum has interesting collections on the history, archaeology and ethnology of Singapore and South-East Asia. On display are the flora and fauna of Singapore, archaeological finds and a valuable collection of Malay arts and crafts.

The Art Gallery displays pictures and decorative art by local artists. There is a collection of coins with exhibits from the 11th c. to the present day.

The Jade Collection was assembled and bequeathed to the state by the brothers Aw Boon Haw (the "Tiger") and Aw Boon Par (the "Leopard"), who made a fortune from their Tiger Balm medicine (see Haw Par Villa and the Facts and Figures, Famous People). Earlier it was housed in the brothers' residence.
 The treasures on display include 384 pieces of jade, valuable Chinese porcelain and Italian marble statues. The collection is one of the finest of its kind in the whole of South-East Asia.

**Location**
Stamford Road

**Bus** 7, 13, 14, 16, 124, 167, 168, 171, 173, 174, 182, 850, CBD 1

**MRT** Dhoby Ghaut

**Opening times**
9am–5.30pm
(closed Monday)

★Jade Collection

## National Stadium                                                        B 6

The National Stadium of Singapore, on Jalan Besar, covers an area of 60ha/150 acres and can accommodate 50,000 visitors. It cost 50 million Singapore dollars to construct. In addition to the usual facilities for both indoor and outdoor sports there are judo rooms, squash courts and tennis and badminton courts. All the facilities provided are in line with Olympic

**Location**
Jalan Besar

**Bus**
14, 16

standards. Associated with the Stadium is a sports medicine research centre. Included in the complex are restaurants, exhibition rooms and a small theatre.

## National University — A 1

**Location**
Kent Ridge/Bukit Timah Hill

**Bus** 33

**MRT**
Ghim Moh

The University of Singapore was founded in 1905 as King Edward VII College; now known as the National University of Singapore, it has facilities covering arts, science and technology and ranks with the best universities in the world.

The main part of the University is at Kent Ridge, in the western part of the island. It has a fine art collection and a large library.

## Padang — D 4

**Location**
St Andrew's Road

**Bus**
CBD 1

**MRT**
City Hall

Padang is the Malay word for plain or open space, and is applied in any South-east Asian town to an area or space which has played a central part in its history and is still the centre of the town's life.

When Stamford Raffles first stepped ashore here in 1819 he had to make his way through a dense mangrove swamp, undeterred by the human skulls which littered the ground – macabre relics of the activities of the pirates of the South China Sea. The first area of open ground which could be traversed without the aid of a bush knife was the open space now known as the Padang, which became the cradle of modern Singapore.

Once the parade ground of British troops, it has long been the meeting-place of Singapore society. The Padang is now the scene of parades by Singapore's military forces, youth organisations and sport associations on

*National University of Singapore*

the republic's National day (August 9th). The annual parades held here on the Queen's Birthday came to an abrupt end in 1942 with the Japanese occupation of Singapore, and even after the Japanese surrender in 1945 things were never quite the same again.

Round the Padang are monuments recalling the days of colonial rule – the Raffles statue in Empress Place, the Victoria Memorial Hall and Theatre, Parliament House, City Hall, the Supreme Court and St Andrew's Cathedral (see entries).

## Pasar Malam

See Markets

## Pasir Ris Beach Park

off map

Pasir Ris Beach Park lies in the north-east of Singapore, between Singapore and Malaysia, opposite the island of Pulau Ubin.

The Pasir Ris Beach Park is a huge leisure park with a giant playground for children. It stretches as far as the beach and has tremendous watersports facilities.

**Bus**
23, 19

**MRT**
Pasir Ris

## Peranakan Museum

See Emerald Hill

## Peranakan Place

See Emerald Hill

## Perumal Temple

See Sri Srinivassa Perumal Temple

## Pulau Hantau (island)

off map

The "Ghost Island" (the literal translation of Pulau Hantu) can be reached in just under half an hour by hired boat from Clifford Pier. It has wonderful beaches for swimming and snorkelling. The time for departure can be agreed with the boat's captain.

**Location**
South of Singapore

## Queen Elizabeth Walk

D 4

Named after Queen Elizabeth II and officially called Queen Elizabeth Walk, this was formerly known as the Promenade.

This seafront promenade, below City Hall and with a fine view of the harbour, runs from the Satay Club (Malay street kitchens) to Merlion Park. It is screened by gardens from the busy traffic of Connaught Drive.

Here Stamford Raffles set foot on the soil of Singapore for the first time. There is a monument to him near here, on the Padang (see entry). The small fountain in Queen Elizabeth Walk commemorates the Chinese philanthropist Tan Kim Seng, who financed Chinatown's first water supply. Another

**Location**
Connaught Drive

**Bus**
1, 10, 30, 50, 60, 70, 75, 82, 94, 97, 100, 107, 125, 146, 189

**MRT**
City Hall

monument, which resembles four rockets and popularly known as the Four Chopsticks, commemorates the Resistance leader Lim Bo Seng, who was tortured to death during the Japanese occupation but died with his lips sealed.

A cenotaph commemorates the 124 Singaporeans who died in the First World War.

Queen Elizabeth Walk has lost some of its atmosphere through the construction of the new Hawker Centre, with its air-conditioning and polystyrene tableware, but it is still a popular meeting place for the young people of Singapore.

## Racecourse

See Turf Club

## ★ Raffles City                                                                                       C 4

**Location**
Bras Basah Road

**Bus**
7, 13, 14, 16, 124, 850, CBD 1

**MRT**
City Hall

**Opening times**
9am–10pm

The Raffles City Complex, with the highest hotel tower in the world (about 226m/741ft, 78 floors), dominates the Singapore skyline even if does not enhance its urban development. Behind Raffles City are a giant shopping centre which caters for more discriminating tastes, a 42-floor office block, Singapore' largest congress centre which can accommodate over 5000 clients, Singapore's highest restaurant (on the 69th floor) and two hotels, the Westin Plaza and the Westin Stamford. Raffles Ballroom is the largest hall without pillars in South-East Asia, the self-supporting ceiling covers 2237sq.m/24,146sq.ft.

Some notable contemporary works of art are integrated into the plain architectural background, the relief of oriental fruits by Don Moulton, the "3 Blue Discs", a giant mobile by Alexander Calder, an aluminium sculpture by Ellsworth Kelly and works by the famous Chinese painter Liu Hai Zu (Cherry Blossom) and Zao Wu Ki.

Below, directly at the base of the huge complex is the Raffles Hotel (see Raffles Hotel), Singapore's most famous hotel.

## Raffles Monument

See Empress Place

## ★ Raffles Hotel                                                                                      C 4

**Location**
Beach Road

**Bus**
7, 14, 16, CBD 1

**MRT**
City Hall

**Name and history**

The "Rafffles" is one of the last nostalgic symbols of Britain's colonial era in Singapore. It ranks among the most famous and traditional of the former British colonial hotels which are still in operation – comparable, perhaps, with "The Peninsula" in Hong Kong. Not only English Queens and Governors stayed here, but also celebrated writers such as Somerset Maugham, Rudyard Kipling and Noel Coward, who was said to have written his novel "Mad dogs and Englishmen go out in the Midday Sun" here. Some hotel suites have been named after certain famous writers.

When Sir Stamford Raffles gave his name to the hotel it was still surrounded by jungle. The last tiger was seen here in 1902 (some stories say it was an escaped tiger from the zoo). In "The Singapore Story" Noel Barber (1978) writes: "That was the birth of the Raffles Hotel, the hotel with the most nostalgic name in the world". The building was later bought and

*Raffles City – the modern face of Singapore* ▶

# Raffles Hotel

enlarged by three Armenian brothers called Sarkie who made it the focus of Singapore's social life. Its fame was immortal. The "London Sphere" called it the "Singapore Savoy". When Somerset Maugham stayed there he said "it represents all the myths of the exotic Orient", whereas Kipling gave more down-to-earth advice: "When in Singapore eat at Raffles". Kipling did not mention that it was also advisable to exercise caution. Only a year or two before his stay, in 1902, Mr M. C. Phillips, director of the neighbouring Raffles Institute, was playing billiards in "Raffles" when a sudden, mighty roar caused him to miss-hit the ball into the wrong pocket. A tiger was under the billiard table.

**Present and future**

However, much has changed since the barman Ngiam Tong Boon invented the "Singapore Sling" in 1915, a cocktail which present-day travellers to Singapore must include in their itinerary.

Despite occupancy rates of 99.3%, which hotel managers elsewhere in the world can only dream about, the "Raffles" was, like many other reminders of the British Empire, in danger of being demolished. After protracted negotiations it was decided "just" to renovate the building with an investment of 150 million US $.

Since 1991, after a three-year refurbishment, the hotel has been attracting travellers who seek nostalgia. The attempt to recreate the atmosphere of the colonial era has been unsuccessful. The old worn cane chairs have been replaced and a luxurious interior created – all that remain are the Indian porters, sweating under their tropical topees, and the barmen serving Stengah (whisky and soda) and the famous "Singapore Sling" (which now, owing to the high number of visitors, unfortunately comes ready-mixed in a container . . .).

But the revived luxury of the "Raffles" will be out of the reach of the average visitor. The 104 suites cost from 600 S-$ upwards (per night) – the hotel guests, who can afford or wish to pay these prices, are kept well away from the normal stream of visitors. They are led into the annexes, along

*Singapore's legendary Raffles Hotel*

sober shopping arcades to expensive restaurants. For the visitor in search of its nostalgic past a small museum contains pictures and documents relating to the venerable "Raffles".

Standard recipe: 3cl gin, 1cl cherry brandy (or cherry liqueur), 1cl Bénédictine D.O.M., half a lime.
 Preparation: half fill a tumbler with crushed ice, squeeze the lime over it. Add the gin, cherry brandy (or cherry liqueur) and Bénédictine. Stir and serve with a straw.
 Alternative: 5cl gin, 3cl of pineapple juice, dash of Cointreau, dash of Angostura Bitter, dash of Bénédictine D.O.M., juice of a lemon, soda water. Preparation: Fill the cocktail shaker one third full with ice, add the spirits, pineapple and lemon juice, shake well. Dilute with soda water and sieve into a cocktail glass.

"Singapore Sling" recipe

## Raffles Place

D 4

Raffles Place has long been one of Singapore's more exclusive shopping areas. The fabrics, the jewellery, the optical and electronic goods and the watches sold in this area cater for the more discerning tastes, which must be accompanied by a correspondingly well-filled wallet or flexible credit card.

Bus
7, 14, 16, CBD 1

MRT
Raffles Place

## Saint Andrew's Cathedral

D 4

The Anglican Cathedral of St Andrew is in the middle of a beautiful park. It was built by Indian prisoners last century (1856–61) and its neo-Gothic style with its tall stained-glass windows give it the appearance of an English village church. The original church was designed by the architect G. D. Coleman (1835) who was well known in Singapore.
 James Thurnbull Thomson designed a new church in 1842 which had a tower. In 1855 this building was demolished and the present-day church erected, to plans by Wing Commander Ronald MacPherson.
 Inside the Cathedral there is a memorial to Sir Stamford Raffles erected in 1861. There was a popular belief, which is still not forgotten, that the ghosts of the former owners, who had their land seized, haunt the site and can only be appeased by an offering of 30 human heads.

Location
Coleman Street/
Saint Andrew's
Road

Bus
124, 173, 174

MRT
City Hall

## Saint John's Islands

off map

After sailing through the Straits of Malacca on February 6th 1819 Stamford Raffles made his first landing in these islands, before crossing over to the main island of Singapore with a small advance party.
 The islands, which are occupied by Malay fishermen, are very popular with bathers.

Boats
From the World
Trade Centre/
Ferry

## Sakya Muni Buddha Gaya Temple

See Temple of 1000 lights

## Science Centre

See Jurong Town, Singapore Science Centre

**Seletar Reservoir**

*St Andrew's Cathedral (See page 83)*

## Seletar Reservoir                                                        off map

**Location**
Mandai Lake Road

**Bus**
137, 171

**Note**

Like the MacRitchie Reservoir (see entry), the Seletar Reservoir has been developed as a recreation centre. It is Singapore's largest reservoir, with a capacity of almost 24,000 million litres/5300 million gallons.

There is an outlook tower which affords magnificent views of the surrounding area.

Singapore's Zoological Gardens (see Zoological Gardens) are close by.

## ★★Sentosa Island                                                           G 1

**Bus**
65, 143, 167

**Ferry**
From the World
Trade Centre
daily 7.30am–10pm
every 15 minutes

**Cablecar**
From Mount Faber
daily 9am–9pm

**Admission fee**

Formerly known as Pulau Blakang Mati, the island was occupied during the British colonial period by forts, but after the British withdrawal (1967) it was developed as a resort island under the more attractive name of Sentosa ("tranquillity"). It now attracts something like a million visitors every year, mostly from the indigenous population, which explains why the island is called "Singapore's playground". Sentosa has become a kind of Asian Disneyland but it still has several attractions for the more demanding visitor.

Sentosa can be reached by cablecar from Mount Faber (see Mount Faber) stopping at the World Trade Centre, offering the visitor a truly breathtaking view of Singapore. A ferry service operates between the World Trade Centre and the Sentosa Ferry Terminal. A bridge was built in 1992 between the World Trade Centre and Sentosa, but this is for the use of buses and taxis only.

A monorail runs round the main features of interest on the island, offering superb views of the scenery and introducing visitors to the topography and vegetation of the tropical world – swamps, mangrove forests, crocodile pools and the biotopes of the coastal regions.

## Sentosa Island

There are also buses operating at 10 minute intervals daily between the main places of interest. Bicycles can be hired from the arrival terminal.

On Sentosa there are numerous restaurants and fast food stalls and overnight accommodation is available in reasonably priced chalets. The visitor can also enjoy the luxury of an international hotel (Baufort group) in the resort (another hotel belonging to the Shangri-la chain is under construction).

Food and Accommodation

There is a camping site where tents can be hired.

Camping

The island's sports and recreation facilites include a roller-skating rink and two 18-hole golf courses.
  Swimming is possible from Tanjong Beach, Central Beach and Siloso Beach (boats, surfboards, sun beds and parasols can all be hired).

Sport and recreation facilities

At the east end of the lagoon there is a boating marina where rowing boats and sailing boats are for hire daily between 9am and 5pm.

Boat marina

Every evening concerts and cultural events take place and there is also a discothèque and a night market.

Evening emtertainment

## Terminal

The new terminal, built in 1920s colonial style, gives the island a rather grandiose sea front and is an attraction in itself.

### Sentosa Island

*Sentosa Island: monorail . . .*

## Musical Fountain

Adjoining the terminal are the Fountain Gardens with a 22m/72ft-high computerised musical fountain and the amphitheatre in the background.

The colourful musical show takes place weekdays and Sundays at 7.30, 8, 8.30 and 9pm and on Saturdays at 7.30, 8, and 8.30pm.

## Sentosa Riverboat

At the new terminal the Sentosa riverboat is a restaurant designed like a Mississippi Paddleboat.

## Maritime Museum

The Maritime Museum illustrates the development of the port of Singapore and boat building in South-East Asia. It has exhibits of historic and modern fishing techniques demonstrating both modern deep-sea fishing equipment and traditional fishing (see Kelongs). It is open daily from 9am–6pm.

## Coralarium

The Coral Museum covers an area of 1.2ha/½ acre with a variety of exhibits from the undersea world of the South China Sea: fishes, shellfish and coral.

## Dari Laut (Shell Collection)

Dari Laut is one of the largest shell collections in the world (open: daily from 9am–6pm).

**Sentosa Island**

*. . . and silver sand*

## Art Centre

The collection displayed in the Art Centre includes contemporary oil-painting, Chinese sculpture, batik-work and pottery from South-East Asia. The gallery is open daily to visitors from 9am–6pm.

## Wax Museum (in the Pioneers and Surrender Chambers Museum)

In the Wax Museum, part of the Pioneers and Surrender Chambers Museum, 27 life-size figures (including models of Lord Louis Mountbatten and General Seishiro Itagki) bring to life the Japanese surrender after the Second World War, while the 1942 surrender of the British to the Japanese is represented by 15 figures.
   In addition there are various scenes depicting life in colonial Singapore.

## Fort Siloso

Fort Siloso, built in 1880, is one of the last of Singapore's coastal fortifications still preserved. During the Second World War the Japanese used it as a prisoner-of-war camp. It contains an interesting Gun Museum.

## Butterfly Park

There is a museum dedicated to the insect world of South-East Asia. In addition to the preserved specimens of this outstanding collection there are more than 4000 live butterflies from 50 different species in a large adjoining area.

## Rare Stone Museum

The Rare Stone Museum contains more than 4000 exhibits, many naturally formed and some cut by hand into bizarre shapes (open: daily 9am–7pm).

**Serangoon Market**

*Moment of surrender, Wax Museum, Sentosa Island*

## Underwater World

One of the main attractions is the largest oceanarium in Asia, the "Underwater World". The visitor steps under a glass dome through a massive sea aquarium with coral gardens, fish (including sharks) and other sea creatures.

For children there is a "Touch Pool" where they can touch living sea creatures.

## Asian Cultural Village

The latest attraction on Sentosa is an Asian village, built directly on the water. It comprises three small villages each representing through the architecture and cultural activities a different part of Asia. Artists and craftsmen produce more or less authentic items from different regions of the continent – in front of the visitor, of course.

There are also all kinds of amusements, for example, the "Mystery Mine", the "Tuk Tuk Jam" or the "Pirate Ship" (open: daily 10am–9pm).

## Serangoon Market

See Markets

## Siloso Beach

See Sentosa Island

**Singapore Science Centre**

## Singapore River

D 1–4

The 3km/2mile long Singapore River flows into the South China Sea. Thanks to its strategic situation the river, which was the island's first harbour and now leads into Keppel Harbour (see entry), is the scene of constant activity as a market and trading centre on the water.

**Bus** CBD 1, 124, 173, 174

**MRT** Raffles Place

Sir Stamford Raffles, the founder of modern Singapore, landed on its east bank on February 6th 1819, looking for a suitable site for a trading station for the British East India Company (see Empress Place). This important event is marked by a white marble statue.

History

The hundreds and hundreds of sampans, as the boats and junks navigated by "swaylos" are called, which, up until a few years ago, used to tranship goods from and to the warehouses, have now been confined to a special section of Keppel Harbour so that the once so picturesque life on the river has lost much of its charm. This step was, however, necessary to clean up the river and fish are breeding here again.

The Boats Quay promenade is to be preserved in its original form and restored with attractive traditional shops. In the stretches between Boat Quay, Clake Quay and Robertson Quay attempts are being made to bring the river to life again for the indigenous population with water taxis, various sports activities and a new night market (see Markets).

## Singapore Science Centre

See Jurong Town

*City of lights: view across the Singapore River*

## ★★ Siong Lim See Monastery

off map

**Location**
Toa Payoh Housing Estate

**Bus**
64, 65, 92, 106, 111, 118, as far as Dhouby Ghaut, change to 146

**MRT**
Toa Payoh

This Twin Grove of the Lotus Mountain Temple is one of the most magnificent Buddhist temples in South-East Asia.
  Completed in 1908 in traditional Chinese style, it is said to be modelled in some respects on the Imperial Palace in Peking.

At the entrance to the temple are gigantic figures of the Four Kings of Heaven, each treading a demon under foot. They are the divine guardians of the sanctuary, protecting it against all evil that may approach from any of the cardinal points.

Beyond these is the Laughing Buddha, a great favourite with the Singapore Chinese, who do not regard their religion as a matter of deadly seriousness. Beside him is the mighty Wei T'o, defender of the faith.

In the innermost chamber, the holy of holies, is a figure of the Buddha deep in meditation. In the rear hall Kuan Yin, goddess of mercy, watches over the oldest part of the temple, which overlooks tranquil gardens. This small wooden shrine has fine wall paintings. The side altars and recesses have a profusion of works of religious art, notable among them the marble Buddha figures from Thailand.

The temple is rich in good omens and in legends related to them. It is said, for example, that some years ago a poor trishaw-man fell asleep in front of the stone lion at the entrance and dreamed that the lion came to life and told him that he would win a great prize in a lottery: whereupon he bought a ticket and won 140,000 Singapore dollars and was able to return to China a rich man.

## Sisters Island

off map

**Location**
South of Singapore

The bathing beaches of these two islands are reached by hired boat from Clifford Pier (see entry) or Jardine Steps.

The return time can be arranged with the boatsman. Camping is not permitted on the islands.

## ★★ Sri Mariamman Hindu Temple

E 3

**Location**
South Bridge Road

**Bus**
124, 143, 173, 174

**MRT**
Raffles Place

**Picture**
See p. 40

The Hindu Temple of Sri Mariamman was built between 1827 and 1843 by an Indian merchant who came to Singapore in a cargo vessel, the "Indiana". The labour force for its construction was provided by Indian convicts.
  This Hindu temple, the oldest and most important in Singapore, is dedicated to the goddess Mariamman, who is attributed with powers of healing. The brightly painted decorative figures on the gopuram, the five-storey tower above the entrance, is inspired by Hindu temples from south India, which accounts for the dominance of the sacred cow.

The imposing façade with countless small sculptured figures depicts the deeds of the goddess Kali and scenes from Hindu mythology. Every evening at six o'clock the mystical music which accompanies the service is diffused over the surrounding area.
  The interior of the temple, under its richly decorated domes, is a riot of ornament and gilding glorifying a host of Hindu divinities.

*Entrance to Siong Lim See Monastery* ▶

Sri Srinivassa Perumal Temple

In association with the Hindu festival of Thimithi (see Practical Information, Events) the Buddhist festival of penance and thanksgiving takes place around October/November depending on the lunar calendar. In a trance-like condition Hindus walk over a long pit filled with glowing coals and hope for forgiveness. The concentration on prayer stops them feeling any pain.

## ★ Sri Srinivassa Perumal Temple — A 4

**Location**
Serangoon Road

The Sri Srinivassa Perumal Temple, shortened to Perumal Temple, was built in 1855 and is the fourth oldest Hindu temple in Singapore. The craftsmen came from south India.

During the Thaipusam festival (see Practical Information, Events) the procession sets out from the Perumal Temple.

The five-storey tower is richly decorated with figures. The walls and ceiling of the shrine dedicated to Perumal, the god of peace, are painted in bright colours.

## Substation — C 4

**Location**
Armenian Street

**MRT**
City Hall

This centre of youth art and culture was built in 1928 as a power station. Today it serves as a gallery, theatre and workshop for creative artists and sculptors.

Information on the events and activities can be obtained by telephone (tel. 3 37 78 00).

Sultan Mosque: exterior...

... and the faithful at prayer

## ★Sultan Mosque C 5

The mosque was built by the last Sultan of Singapore, Sultan Iskandar Shah. Sir Stamford Raffles, the founder of the city, donated 3000 dollars from his own pocket towards its construction in 1819. The present day mosque was completed in 1928 and is based on Saracen architecture. The design is, however, a hotch-potch of classical, European, Turkish, Arab and Persian features, the product of the imagination of the English architects Swan & Maclaren.

The Sultan Mosque is the religious centre of Singapore's Moslem population. It has 14 entrances to each of which red carpet is laid for Friday prayers.

The interior is decorated with Arabic calligraphy. The floors are of green and gold coloured marble.

**Location**
North Bridge Road/
Arab Street

**Bus**
13

**MRT**
Bugis

**Opening times**
outside of prayer

## Sultan's Tomb

See Fort Canning Rise

## Supreme Court D 4

In a proclamation of 1823 Sir Stamford Raffles declared all men equal in the eyes of the law; and four years later, in 1827, Singapore's first court of law was established in a small bungalow. The present Supreme Court building was brought into use in 1937.

**Location**
St Andrew' Road

**Bus** CBD 1

*Supreme Court*

**Tang Dynasty City**

MRT
City Hall

It occupies the site of the old Europe Hotel, the meeting-place until 1932 of the Singapore elite. The building now houses the municipal administration (City Hall). In Graeco-Roman style, it has a façade lined with slender Corinthian columns and is crowned by a tall and imposing dome.

## ★Tang Dynasty City

off map

**Location**
Jalan Ahmed Ibrahim

**Bus**
From Jurong Interchange 250, 251, 253

**MRT**
Jurong East

**Opening times**
daily
9.30am –6.30pm

**Admission fee**

The idea for the largest historical theme park in Asia came from the desire for Singapore to have its own film studio. So one of Singapore's latest tourist attractions was built on a 12ha/5 acre site at an outlay of about 70 million S $. The Tang Dynasty City in Jurong is a copy of Chang-An, the capital of the Tang (also Xiang) dynasty, which ruled from A.D. 618–906.

Sights include the 65m/213ft-high Pagoda of the Monkey Gods, the underground palace with 1200 terracotta warriors, the Imperial Palace of Emperor Tang Tai Zong and the Travellers Inn.
The park is full of activity. Life in the bygone era is very vividly presented, with the Monkey God, the Emperor and his concubine Yang Kwei-fei making personal appearances.
Nearby the visitor can discover some of the tricks behind the scenes of modern film techniques.

In addition the Tang Dynasty City has exhibition halls and function rooms (with capacity for 20 to 2500 people), three restaurants and a row of shops.

## Tanjong Pagar Road

See Chinatown

*Tang Dynasty City*

Telok Ayer Street

## ★★ Tanjung Pinang

Indonesia

Two hours by boat east of Singapore lies the Riau Archipelago, a group of islands which belongs to Singapore. In contrast with the futuristic Singapore the visitor encounters a completely different world unspoilt by modern development: Malay kampongs (villages), magnificent sandy beaches and coral reefs for diving.

Several times a day the modern ships of the P. T. Pulau Intan Sari depart from Finger Pier in Singapore and arrive at Sekupang harbour, on the island of Batam, about half an hour later. Customs formalities are carried out here. Travellers from Singapore require an individual valid passport. The same ship continues to Tanjung Pinang (1½ hours), the administrative centre of Pulau Bintan island.

The town is reputed to be the smugglers' centre of the archipelago handling all modern electronic and luxury goods which arrive in Indonesia from Singapore. In the harbour the beautiful old bugis sailing boats can be seen.

**Access**
Charter flights from Seletar Airport, Singapore

Ferry from Finger Pier, Singapore

Depart daily 8.15, 10.15am, 12.15, 2.15 and 4.15pm

See Practical Information, Information

**Information**

Modern accommodation can be found in the Holidays Indah and Wisma Riau hotels. For a longer weekend the east coast is to be recommended, particularly the traditional wood-built Trikora Country Club by the "Blue Lagoon". This can be booked in Singapore at the Trikora Resort Development Pte. Ltd., 545 Orchard Road, 4–27 Far East Shopping Centre, tel. 2 35 86 11. Apart from the beautiful sandy beach facilities include hire of diving equipment, boat hire, a golf course, squash and tennis courts.

**Hotels**

The rural countryside of the island can be explored by hire car and a trip by boat to the islands of Senggarang and Penyengat off the west coast is worthwhile.

**Senggarang Penyengat**

In Senggarang there are three Chinese temples from the 17th c. A 300-year old temple and the Sultan's Mosque, a gift from the Sultan of Singapore in 1832, can be seen on Penyengat.

At the end of 1988 the Turi Beach Resort was opened in Batam on the northern tip of the island. It was built in traditional style and offers a variety of recreational and entertainment facilities.

**Batam**

## ★ Tan Si Chong Su Temple

D 3

The Tan Si Chong Su Temple is also known as Tan Seng Haw Temple or Po Chiak Kung Temple. It is a national monument dating from 1876.

**Location**
Magazine Road

The temple of the Tan clan with a view over the Singapore River has outstanding examples of wood carving in the Minnan style. Nearly all the building material was brought by boat or junk from China.

**Bus**
123, 139, 143

**MRT**
Somerset

The Tan Si Chong Temple is the meeting place of Singapore's Tan community.

## ★ Telok Ayer Street

E 3

This street, which once ran along the sea but is now further inland as a result of land deposition, has some fine well preserved old buildings, particularly the religious shrines from old Chinatown.

**Location**
Chinatown

**Temple of 1000 Lights**

*Telok Ayer Street: the charm . . .         . . . of old Singapore*

**Bus**
97, 125, 130, 131

**MRT**
Raffles Place

First comes the Fuk Tak Ch'i Temple (see entry) from 1820, then the Ying Fo Fui Kun, a shrine and the Guild House of the Hakka. On the other side of the junction with Cross Street the Hok Teck Ch'i Temple dating from 1824 is of interest.

Past Boon Tan Street is the Nagore Durgha Shrine (see entry), the Masjid Chulia, an example of the south Indian Islamic tradition from 1828. Finally there are the pretty Thian Hok Keng Temple (see entry) and the Al-Abrar Mosque of the Tamil Muslims

Telok Ayer Street is one of the few streets in Singapore to have retained its old charm.

## Telok Ayer Market

**Location**
Boon Tat Street

Telok Ayer Market is located in a cast iron building, the last of its kind in South-East Asia. For many years the fish market, established in 1894, and later the vegetable market was the meeting place of Singapore housewives.

Today, following thorough renovation, it is a cultural and culinary meeting place. There are regular theatre performances, pantomimes, concerts and spontaneous acts, apart from the many restaurants and foodstalls. It has remarkable filigree wrought iron decoration. Much of this handsome building was prefabricated in Glasgow, shipped to Singapore and reassembled.

## ★★Temple of 1000 Lights (Sakya Muni Buddha Gaya Temple)     A 4

**Location**
Race Course Road

When the young Buddhist monk Vutthisasara came to Singapore from his native Siam (Thailand) he resolved to build a temple to honour the Buddha, the Enlightened One.

*Temple of 1000 Lights*

In the mid 1970s he died at the age of 94, his life's work accomplished: the Temple of a Thousand Lights was completed, and he had spread his doctrines of the Buddha in Singapore by his preaching.

The temple has as its central figure a huge seated Buddha, some 15m/50ft high and weighing 300 tons, which is surrounded after dark by a nimbus of lights, said to number a thousand.

Round the base of the figure are scenes from the life of the Buddha, and the temple contains a precious relic, a piece of bark from the bodhi tree under which the Buddha attained Enlightenment. There is also mother-of-pearl replica of the Buddha's footprint, copied from the one on Adam's Peak in Sri Lanka (Ceylon). The entire temple, down to the tigers guarding the gate, was built by Vutthisasara with his own hands.

**Bus**
23, 64, 65, 106, 111, 198

**Opening times**
9am–4.30pm

## ★★Thian Hok Keng Temple

E 3

Thian Hok Keng, the Temple of Heavenly Happiness, is Singapore's oldest Chinese temple, built in 1840 as a resting-place and hostel for Chinese immigrants from Hokkien province.

The temple is dedicated to Ma-chu-po, Mother of Heavenly Sages in Chinese mythology. In earlier days every Chinese junk carried a small shrine in honour of the goddess. The temple is still a resting place for Chinese seamen, dockworkers and old coolies. It has rich carved ornament and fine lacquer-painting.

It is laid out along the traditional north–south axis. Both the building material and the craftsmen came from China. The splendid dragon columns at the entrance are each worked from a single piece of granite. In the main hall are the altars of Ma-chu-po and the sages Tien Hou, Shakyamuni and Confucius. In the courtyard, in the temple of success is the statue of Fa Zhu Gong, the god of justice.

**Location**
Telok Ayer Street

**Bus**
CBD 1

**MRT**
Raffles Place

**Tiger Balm Gardens**

*Elaborate carving, Thian Hok Keng Temple*

## Tiger Balm Gardens

See Haw Par Villa

## Tua Pek Kong Temple

See Kusu Island

## Turf Club
**off map**

**Location**
Bukit Timah Road

**Bus**
171, 173, 174, 182

**Times of race-meetings**
See newspapers

Horses came to Singapore with the British, and the new sport of horse-racing made its début about 130 years ago. Not surprisingly, perhaps, for the Chinese passion for gambling and for competing comes second only to their interest in eating.

Wealthy Chinese businessmen, Malay princes and the British colony became members of the Turf Club of Singapore, on whose racecourse the much-sought-after Singapore Cup is still contested every year.

The stud farms of Singapore and Malaysia are world-famed, being particularly noted for breeding horses which can stand up to the tropical climate. During the race-meetings millions of dollars are staked, part of the money going into the legal lottery and thus into the state coffers, but some of it also going to line the pockets of the illicit bookmakers who batten onto the sport. Everyone bets, from well-to-do businessmen to respectable Chinese amahs (nurses or maids).

## Zoological Gardens

This is still a happy hunting ground of the Chinese secret societies (thongs), of which there are officially reported to be 37, divided into something like a hundred gangs. In 1959 it was estimated that some 60 per cent of all Singaporeans were connected with one or other of these societies, which are nowadays mainly involved in illegal betting and lotteries but which also dominate the lush night light of Singapore.

## Underwater World

See Sentosa Island

## ★Van Kleef Aquarium  C/D 3

This small aquarium contains some 4600 sea creatures of all kinds, including rare specimens from many parts of the world. Among them are the local "flame fish", sea anemones, coral fish, polyps, king crabs, turtles and sea snakes. Also of great interest are the various species of marine flora and corals.

The aquarium, originally based on the private collection of a former resident of Singapore, Mr K. van Kleef, was established in its present form in Central Park (see Fort Canning Park) in 1955.

Singapore is now one of the world's largest exporters of aquarium fishes and other sea creatures. A large firm dealing in aquarium specimens has its headquarters in the Central Building, and there are other aquarium shops in the surrounding area.

**Location**
Central Park

**Bus**
123, 143

**MRT**
Dhoby Ghaut

**Opening times**
daily 9.30am–9pm

**Admission fee**

## Victoria Memorial Hall and Victoria Theatre  D 4

At Empress Place (see entry) the Victoria Memorial Hall and the Victoria Theatre are to be found, built in the mid-19th c. and early 20th c. in classical style and named after the British Queen Victoria. The clock tower of the Memorial Hall is one of Singapore's emblems.
   The Victoria Theatre was originally the town hall in Singapore's early days. Today the Singapore Sinfonia Orchestra (see Practical Information, Concerts) performs concerts in the Memorial Hall.
   The Memorial Hall is opposite the Supreme Court (see entry).

**Location**
High Street

**Bus**
CBD 1

**MRT**
City Hall

## Wax Museum

See Sentosa Island

## ★★Zoological Gardens

Laid out in 1973 Singapore's Zoological Gardens are one of the greatest zoos in the world. They are a must not only for families with children but for every visitor to Singapore. Over 1600 animals in enclosures resembling their natural habitat offer an enchanting glimpse into the fauna of South-East Asia. An electric railcar runs through the park.
   Opening times: daily 8.30am–6pm.

Great importance is attached to the way in which the animals are kept, instead of expensive cages, which are only there in high-risk areas, natural

**Location**
Mandai Lake Road

**Bus**
131, 171

**Admission fee**

## Zoological Gardens

*Perfect manners: Orang-utangs at Singapore Zoo*

barriers have been erected the same as the animals are used to in the wild. Much effort also goes into breeding rare species.

**Breakfast with the animals**

The visitor is offered the opportunity to have breakfast (daily at 10.30am) or tea (daily at 2.30pm) together with the animals. It is even possible to have breakfast alone with the tame female orang-utan Ah Meng by booking in advance (tel. 2 69 34 11).

**Night zoo**

From the beginning of 1994 a unique attraction has been the new night zoo costing about 60 million S-$. On a site of 40ha/16 acres, which has been created with sensitivity for the natural landscape, 1200 animals, some of them threatened with extinction, can be observed. Jungle, mountain and savannah habitats have been recreated here for the animals (giraffes, jackals, water buffalo, porcupines, fish otters and many others) which have been brought here from all over the world.

The 3.2km/2 mile-trip around the zoo by small train takes about three-quarters of an hour or else it can be walked in a good two hours. An ingenious lighting system has been developed so that the animals are visible – at least the owners maintain this to be the case – but not disturbed.

*Apothecary's shop in Singapore's Chinatown* ▶

# Practical Information

The sign # before an address indicates a combined number giving the floor or storey in a highrise block or large building complex.

## Air Travel

Most of Singapore's visitors arrive by air at its ultra-modern international airport on the Changi Peninsula. Over 50 international airlines fly regular services to and from Singapore and there are direct flights from many cities in Europe, North America and other English-speaking countries, including scheduled flights by Singapore Airlines (SIA) to 52 cities throughout the world, among them Auckland, London Heathrow, Los Angeles, Melbourne, Perth, San Francisco and Sydney.

## Airport

**Changi Airport**

Singapore's international Changi Airport (see A–Z) handles over 15 million passengers a year through its two terminals, each large enough to take twice as many.
Facilities in both terminal complexes include restaurants and bars, banks, money-changing, offices for hotel reservation and tour booking desks, car-hire desks, post offices, telecommunication services (phoning is free within Singapore), tourist information centre and left-luggage lockers. Passengers can shop in the duty-free stores on both arrival (but no tobacco items) and departure.

**Transit passengers**

Transit passengers with more than four hours in hand can leave their baggage in the 24-hour left-luggage office and take a free city tour from the airport courtesy of the Singapore Tourist Promotion Board (see Sightseeing).

**Getting to the city centre**

Changi Airport is on the island's network of expressways and it takes about half an hour to get to the city centre by taxi or car. Hotel buses (tickets in the arrival hall) also take passengers between the airport and many of the hotels.

**Departure tax**

All passengers must pay an airport tax on departure from Singapore. This is less for flights to Brunei and Malaysia. Airport tax coupons can also be bought in advance at hotels, travel agencies and airline offices.

**Check-in times**

Passengers leaving on intercontinental flights must check in at least an hour and a half beforehand or risk allowing the airline to re-allocate their places. For local destinations only an hour is necessary.

**Transfers**

Allow two hours for transfers between international flights.

**Confirmation of return flights**

As a general rule return or onward flights must be reconfirmed with the airline in question 48 hours before departure. For charter flights this is the responsibility of the tour operator's local representative, but on scheduled flights it is up to the individual. Again, failure to do so can result in the airline re-allocating the ticket. Confirmation is particularly important around festivals and holidays such as Christmas and the Chinese New Year when every single seat will be taken on most flights.

*Control Tower at Singapore's Changi Airport* ▶

**Air Travel**

*Boeing 747–400 belonging to Singapore Airlines*

Flight enquiries	Tel. 1800–542 44 22/542 69 88
1800–542 12 34

# Airlines

As many as 57 international airlines operate scheduled services to Singapore, including Singapore Airlines and its subsidiary Silk Air (formerly Tradewinds) which primarily serves nearby destinations in south-east Asia. For any airlines not included in the following list check under the appropriate section of the Yellow Pages.

Air France
1 Tanglin Road 01–01, Ming Court Shopping Arcade; tel. 737 63 55

Alitalia
15–05 Wisma Atria, 435 Orchard Road; tel. 737 31 66

British Airways
02–16 The Paragon, 290 Orchard Road; tel. 253 84 44

Garuda Indonesian Airways
01–68 United Square, 101 Thomson Road; tel. 250 28 88

KLM Royal Dutch Airlines
01–02 Mandarin Hotel, 333 Orchard Road; tel. 737 76 22

Lauda Air
140 Cecil Street #08–03; tel. 226 12 66

Lufthansa
390 Orchard Road, #05–07, Palais Renaissance; tel. 737 92 22

Malaysian Airways System (MAS)
02–09 Singapore Shopping Centre, 190 Clemenceau Avenue;
tel. 336 67 77

Philippine Airlines
01–022 Parklande Shopping Mall, 35 Selegie Road;
tel. 336 16 11

Quantas
01–05 Mandarin Hotel, 333 Orchard Road; tel. 737 37 44

Silk Air
c/o Tradewinds Pte Ltd., 77 Robinson Road; tel. 221 22 21

Singapore Airlines
77 Robinson Road 01–06;
tel. 223 88 88
Mandarin Hotel, Orchard Road;
tel. 229 72 93/4
North Bridge Road, Raffles City Shopping Centre;
tel. 229 72 74

Swissair
435 Orchard Road, #18–01, Wisma Atria;
tel. 737 81 33

Thai Airways International
133 Cecil Street, #08–01; tel. 224 99 77
Keck Seng Towers; tel. 224 99 77

## Flight Packages

There is keen competition in Singapore among the big international tour operators (see Travel Agencies), who offer all kinds of air travel packages, so it pays to shop around and compare prices. Both Singapore Airlines and Malaysian Airlines offer good deals on flights to destinations in south-east Asia. | Tour operators

The national airlines of Singapore, Malaysia, Thailand, Indonesia and the Philippines produce a combined circular tour package of flights at bargain prices between their countries. | Circular tours

Singapore Airlines and Malaysian Airlines both operate 40-minute flights between Singapore and Kuala Lumpur. The shuttle flights on a first come, first served basis are particularly good value. For further information contact the airlines. See also Getting to Singapore. | Flights to Malaysia

## Antiques

Singapore is one of south-east Asia's largest markets for antiques. These can range from the ethnic art of the region's many native peoples to antique jewellery and Chinese furniture and porcelain.

Although most of the Far East's other countries have strict controls governing the export of antiques, there is no problem about exporting items originating in Singapore. | Export
   Anyone taking Asian antiques bought in Singapore with them on to other countries in the Far East should get an import certificate on entering the other country in order to avoid any difficulties when leaving again.

All the top international hotels have antique shops – with prices to match – as do shopping centres and department stores (see entries) and there is a large concentration of them along Orchard Road. | Antique shops

**Beaches**

The competition is fierce and it is worth comparing prices in order to be able to strike a hard bargain. Antique shops in Singapore include:

Antiques of the Orient Pte Ltd., 19 Tanglin Road, #02–40 Tanglin Shopping Centre

China Crafts Pte Ltd., 545 Orchard Road. #03–08 Far East Shopping Centre

D'Antiquemart Pte Ltd., 36 Watten Rise

Karenny Norman Pte Ltd., 176 Orchard Road, #01–40 Centrepoint

L'Orient Shopping Arcade, Westin Plaza Hotel Lobby, 2/4 Stamford Road

Michelangelo Pte Ltd., 400 Orchard Road, #03–07 Orchard Towers

Moongate, 19 Tanglin Road, B 1–22–23 & 24, Tanglin Shopping Centre

Oriental Souvenirs, 252 North Bridge Road, #02–26 Raffles City Shopping Centre

Singapore Souvenirs Pte Ltd., 304 Orchard Road, #B1–10 Lucky Plaza

Supreme Gift Shop, 22 Orange Grove Road, Shangri-La Hotel

Tien Kee Brothers (Bali House) Pte Ltd., 27 Middle Road

Uni-Q Connoisseurs' Gift Boutique, 19 Tanglin Road, #03–32 Tanglin Shopping Centre

Other antique shops can be found in the Yellow Pages under Antique Dealers.

Unless you are a real expert always get professional advice before buying anything very expensive since Singapore is famous for its copies.

## Beaches

There are good bathing beaches on Sentosa Island (see A–Z) and the southern islands. East Coast Park and Changi Beach (see A–Z, East Coast Park Lagoon, Changi Beach) also offer plenty of opportunities for water sports and swimming. It is also worth making the trip to Malaysia for beaches such as those at Desaru or on the islands of Sibu, Tioman and Pulau Hantu (see A–Z, Pulau Hantu).

## Boat Cruises

One of the best ways to see Singapore is from the water and there are plenty of cruises both close to the island and further afield.

| | |
|---|---|
| Harbour cruises | Daily at 10.30am, 12.30, 2.30, 3, and 4pm, from Clifford Pier and the World Trade Centre and lasting about 2½ hours. |
| Singapore River cruises | Daily from 9am to 10.30pm half-hourly by bumboat from North Boat Quay, Raffles Place and Clarke Quay. |
| Dinner cruises | Dinner cruises in vessels including a Chinese junk: daily at 6, 6.30, 7 and 9pm, lasting between 1½ and 2½ hours and including dinner on board, from Clifford Pier and World Trade Centre by operators such as Eastwind (tel. 533 34 32) and Watertours (tel. 533 98 11). |

A number of tour operators offer cruises around the Southern Islands of Kusu, Saint John's Islands (see A–Z), Sisters and Lazarus, but anyone wanting to make the trip on their own can take the ferry from the World Trade Centre. — Island cruises

For chartered and regional cruises and day-trips and weekend trips to other islands to the north and the south of Singapore enquire at the harbour, the Singapore Tourist Promotion Board (see Information), or local travel agencies (see entry).

A catamaran service to Malacca runs throughout the working week and takes about 4½ hours. There are also ferries from Changi Point to Desaru, as well as a number of package tours. — To Malaysia

## Bus trips

Malaysia is only a 30-minute bus ride away over the Causeway from Singapore, and many of Singapore's tour operators offer a broad choice of coach trips to Malaysian destinations. — To Malaysia

Fares are generally quite cheap. Scheduled express coaches depart daily for the following destinations: — Coach services

From Lavender Street terminal
Butterworth: daily at 6.30am; duration 7–8 hours
Kuala Lumpur: daily at 9am, 1 and 10pm; duration about 7 hours
Penang: daily at 6.30am; duration 5 hours
Malacca: 8, 9, 10, and 11am, 2, 3, and 4pm; duration about 4½ hours
Kuantan: 9, 10am and 10pm; travel time 3–4 hours

From Bansan Street terminal
Johor Bahru: 6.30am–midnight every 7 minutes; duration about 40 minutes

The 170 bus, which runs from Queen Street or Bukit Timah Road every 15 minutes, also goes to Johor Bahru.

## Camping

There are no campsites in Singapore except on Sentosa Island (see A–Z) where there are tents for hire. Camper vehicles are not allowed into the country unless for trans-shipment.

## Car rental

Exploring Singapore in a hire-car can be a real pleasure, especially for those used to driving on the left. Rental cars can also be taken into Malaysia and handed over in any of the main towns and cities.

Cars can be rented by the day or the week at rates ranging between S$50 and S$200 a day, plus mileage, with special rates for longer periods. Hire-cars can also be pre-booked before arrival. — Rates

Besides the big international names, all of which have branches in Singapore, there is a whole host of local companies providing self-drive cars as well as limousine and chauffeur-driven services. For names and addresses look under Rent a Car in the Yellow Pages. — Car-hire firms

Avis Rent a Car: tel. 737 16 68
Budget Enterprise: tel. 222 23 55

**Chemists**

|  | Hertz Rent a Car: tel. 734 46 46
National Car Rental: tel. 338 84 44
San's Tours & Car Rentals: tel. 734 99 22
Sintat Rent a Car: tel. 295 22 11 |
|---|---|
| Documents | Hire-car drivers must be over 23 and be able to produce their national driving licence or a valid international driving licence. |
| Insurance | Like everyone else in Singapore drivers of hire-cars must have third-party insurance. All-risk cover can also be obtained at extra cost. |
| Breakdowns | See Motoring |

## Chemists

See Health Care

## Chinese Street Opera

**Information**
Tourist Information
tel. 334 13 35

Chinese street opera, or "wayang" as it is called by the Chinese who first brought it here from the Chinese mainland, is very much part of the Singapore street scene (see Culture), especially around Chinatown during the Festival of the Hungry Ghosts in July/August (see Events).

This telling of legends and historical events re-enacting tales of love, loyalty, death and betrayal, and the deeds of heroes and warriors is performed within the colourful setting of temporary stages where garishly made-up actors in the traditional lavish costumes use music and dance, mime and recitation, ritual gestures, song and acrobatics to tell their story.

*A traditional Chinese opera*

## Cinema

Singapore has 42 cinemas with a total seating capacity of 48,000. The feature films are all imported, and come from Taiwan and Hong Kong (Chinese dialogue), India, Indonesia and Malaysia (Tamil), the USA, Britain and Italy (English). Consequently most are sub-titled in one or even two languages. For programme details consult the daily press or Singapore Tourist Promotion Board publications (see Information).

## Clothing

Singapore is some 135km/84 miles north of the Equator and average daytime temperatures are around 30°C/86°F, with the nights only very slightly cooler, so light summer clothing is called for. With this level of humidity synthetics, which are not particularly absorbent, are best avoided, especially as tight-fitting underwear; the best material is cotton. Since most hotels and other buildings are air-conditioned it is wise to carry a light wrap or cardigan when spending some time in, say, a restaurant.

Dress standards in Singapore are very relaxed. Only a few restaurants, including the most exclusive, insist on a jacket and tie. Long-sleeved batik shirts and blouses in reasonably restrained patterns are considered socially acceptable but anyone here on business would do well to wear a collar and tie.

The Singaporeans tend to frown upon too much of a hippy look. The same goes for suggestive T-shirts, and in both instances you can run the risk of coming into conflict with the forces of law and order, possibly as early as on arrival.

During the rainy seasons (December–March, June–September; see Facts and Figures, Climate) it is advisable to bring a lightweight raincoat or an umbrella.

## Conduct and Behaviour

Singapore's form of government is often seen as something of a "Guardian State", a reference to the many campaigns whereby the authorities try to instil high public standards using what to some may appear draconian measures for apparently minor misdemeanours such as large fines for chewing gum or dropping litter. Whatever your views there is no doubt that all this has succeeded in earning Singapore a reputation as the cleanest city in Asia if not the world.

Visitors are just as liable to these fines as any of the locals, so you would do well to take heed of the following strictures if you want to avoid any unpleasant encounters with Singapore's ubiquitous enforcement officers.

Smoking is banned in many public places such as lifts, public transport, taxis, office buildings, theatres, cinemas, sporting venues, air-conditioned restaurants and shopping centres, etc. A casually discarded cigarette-end can earn a fine of as much as S$1000.

*No Smoking*

Gum-chewing in public is not allowed. In fact chewing-gum as such may not even be imported. There is a reason behind this. Not so long ago someone stuck their used gum in the photoelectric cell of a subway door, holding up the whole of the system, so the authorities decided to put a stop to this once and for all and banned importing, selling or chewing gum.

*Chewing gum*

Dropping litter in the street and other public places is liable to fines as high as S$1000.

*Litter*

**Concerts**

*Be warned! Penalties can be severe (St John's Island)*

| | |
|---|---|
| Flushing the toilet | Failure to flush a public toilet after use can also incur a fine, and anyone using a lift as a public lavatory runs the risk of a S$500 fine. |
| Jaywalking | Anyone crossing the street illegally within 50 metres of a pedestrian crossing – the limits are marked by signs of a pedestrian with a line through him – risks a S$50 fine. |

## Concerts

| | |
|---|---|
| Singapore Symphony Orchestra | The Singapore Symphony Orchestra (SSO), founded in 1979, usually stages its concerts in the Victoria Concert Hall (see A–Z, Victoria Memorial Hall and Victoria Theatre). Programmes include European classics and the works of Asian composers, often featuring well-known international conductors and soloists. There are also lunch-time concerts by SSO ensembles. For up-to-date programme information check with the daily press (see Newspapers and Periodicals), the Victoria Concert Hall box office (tel. 339 61 20) or the SSO ticket office (tel. 338 12 30/39). |
| Concerts in the Botanical Gardens | Concerts of works by European and Asian composers take place every Sunday evening at 5.30 in the Botanical Gardens. For further information contact the Singapore Tourist Promotion Board (see Information). |

## Currency

| | |
|---|---|
| Currency | Singapore's unit of currency is the Singapore dollar ($, S$, SID) which is made up of 100 cents (c). |

## Currency

*Singapore banknotes and coins*

Coins are in denominations of 5, 10, 20 and 50 cents and one dollar, and there are banknotes for 1 (being phased out), 5, 10, 20, 50, 100, 500, 1000 and 10,000 dollars. Brunei banknotes will also be accepted in payment but Malaysian currency will not.

Coins and banknotes

Singapore has a free currency market, with dealing in every currency. Money can be changed at any bank, by licensed money changers, and in hotels. Any form of foreign currency can be brought in and there is no limit to the amount.

Currency regulations

Singapore's central bank, the Monetary Authority, has also issued a number of specially minted gold and silver coins. Information about these can be had from banks or the Singapore Mint Pte Ltd. (249, Jalan Boon Lay, Singapore 2261), which sends free quarterly bulletins on request to collectors all over the world.

Special issues

The official exchange rate is fixed daily by the Monetary Authority and published in the business section of the local press (see Newspapers and Periodicals).

Exchange rates

In addition to banks, money can be changed by licensed money changers. These are to be found, duly signed as such, in most shopping centres. They give better rates than the hotels, who charge a commission.

Changing money

The best course is to take travellers' cheques since this is safer and even taking into account the percentage for insurance the rate of exchange often works out better than for cash. The fact that they are insured means it is easier to get them replaced quickly if they are lost or stolen although the cheques must be kept separately from the receipt, otherwise the insurance is invalid.

Travellers' cheques

**Currency**

When changing travellers' cheques you need to present your passport and usually give your hotel address on the form as well. Once you get your receipt be sure to check the stated amount against the cash you receive.

Eurocheques

Eurocheques are not generally accepted as a means of payment in Singapore except by a few European money institutions.

**Credit cards**

Most shops, department stores and shopping centres accept the major international credit cards (Eurocard/Mastercard, American Express, Asia Card, Visa, Carte Blanche, Diners Club, etc.).

Cash machines

Almost all banks have cash machines, here called "Automatic Teller Machines" (ATM), where you can use your card and pin number to withdraw cash.

One bad habit occasionally encountered in Singapore is for the fee which the vendor should pay to the credit card company to be added to the price of the goods. If this should happen let the credit card company know and give them the name of the shop.

Lost
credit cards

Inform the credit card company immediately if your card goes missing.

American Express: tel. 235 81 33
Carte Blanche: tel. 339 29 22
Diners Club: tel. 294 42 22
Eurocard/Mastercard: tel. 533 28 88
Visa: tel. 224 90 33

# Banks

Singapore has 134 operating national and international banks, with a total of 395 branches capable of carrying out every kind of banking transaction. The national equivalent of a central bank is the Monetary Authority of Singapore which sets the daily exchange rate.

Banks in Singapore include the following:

Asia Commercial Bank Ltd., 2 Mistri Road

Banque Nationale de Paris, 20 Collyer Quay,
#01–01 Tung Centre

Bangkok Bank, 180 Cecil Street, Bangkok Bank Building

Bank Negara Indonesia 1946, 3 Malacca Street

Bank of America, 78 Shenton Way

Bank of China, 4 Battery Road

Bank of Singapore, 101 Cecil Street, #01–02

Chase Manhattan Bank, 50 Raffles Place, Shell Tower

Citibank NA, 1 Shenton Way, #06–00 UIC Building

Development Bank of Singapore, 6 Shenton Way,
DBS Building

Hong Kong & Shanghai Bank, 21 Collyer Quay,
Overseas Union House

International Bank of Singapore, 50 Collyer Quay,
#01–01 Ocean Building

Malayan Banking Berhad, 2 Battery Road,
#01–00 Malayan Bank Chambers

Standard Chartered Bank, 6 Battery Road

United Commercial Bank, 140–142 Robinson Road,
#01–00 Chow House

The banks have branches in the arrival and departure halls at the airport and in the main building with 24-hour facilities for changing money. — At the airport

See entry — Opening times

## Customs Regulations

Singapore is basically a free port and as such charges no export duty but for policy reasons it has a number of restrictions on what visitors may bring into the country, although there is no limit on the amount of currency.

Visitors over the age of 18 and arriving from a country other than Malaysia are allowed to bring in 1 litre of spirits, 1 litre of wine or port and 1 litre of beer duty-free for personal consumption, but duty must be paid on tobacco products in line with the Government's anti-smoking policy or they must be left in Customs Bond until departure. This can also be done with other items in quantities above the duty-free limit. In common with many countries Singapore has import controls and restrictions on a number of items and prohibits the entry of several others. — Arrival
 Controlled and restricted items which may be subject to inspection or for which permits are required include arms and explosives, animals, birds and their by-products, meat products and plants with soil, cartridges, pre-recorded cassettes, newspapers, books and magazines, films, videotapes and disks.
 Prohibited items include controlled drugs and psychotropic substances (see Drugs), reproductions of copyright publications, including videos, endangered species and their by-products, and obscene articles and publications, plus chewing gum and newspapers from neighbouring Malaysia.

There is no export duty but export permits are required for items requiring permits on entry as well as precious stones and jewellery other than reasonable personal effects (see also Motoring). — Departure

The duty-free limits for Ireland and the United Kingdom for items purchased outside the European Union are 200 cigarettes or 50 cigars or 250 g tobacco and 1 litre spirits and 2.1 litre wine. The allowances operated by a number of other countries are as follows: Australia 250 cigarettes or 50 cigars or 250 g tobacco, 1 litre spirits or 1 litre wine; Canada 200 cigarettes and 50 cigars and 900 g tobacco, 1.1 litre spirits or wine; New Zealand 200 cigarettes or 50 cigars or 250 g tobacco, 1 litre spirits and 4.5 litres wine; South Africa 400 cigarettes and 50 cigars and 250 g tobacco, 1 litre spirits and 2 litres wine; USA 200 cigarettes and 100 cigars and a reasonable quantity of tobacco, 1 litre spirits or 1 litre wine. — Re-entry to other countries

## Diplomatic Representation

## Representation in Singapore

Australian High Commission — Australia
25 Napier Road; tel. 737 93 11; open: Mon–Fri. 8.30am–4.30pm

**Disabled Access**

| | |
|---|---|
| Canada | Canadian High Commission<br>80 Anson Road, #14–00, IBM Towers;<br>tel. 225 63 63: open: Mon.–Fri. 8am–4pm |
| Ireland | Irish Consulate<br>541 Orchard Road, #08–01 Liat Towers;<br>tel. 733 21 80: open: Mon–Fri. 9am–4pm |
| New Zealand | New Zealand High Commission<br>391A Orchard Road, #15–06 Ngee Ann City Tower A;<br>tel. 235 99 66: open: Mon.–Fri. 8.30am–4.30pm |
| South Africa | 331 North Bridge Road, #15–00 Odeon Towers;<br>tel. 339 33 19: open: Mon.–Fri. 8.30am–1pm, 2–5pm |
| United Kingdom | British High Commission<br>325 Tanglin Road;<br>tel. 473 93 33: open: Mon.–Fri. 8.30am–noon, 4–4.30pm. 8.30am–5pm (telephone enquiries) |
| United States of America | American Embassy<br>30 Hill Street;<br>tel. 338 02 51: open: Mon.–Fri. 8.30am–5.15pm |

For information about Singapore's diplomatic representation abroad consult the nearest representative of the Singapore Tourist Promotion Board (see Information).

## Disabled Access

Singapore is a disability-friendly city, where the authorities have gone to great lengths to make access for the disabled a priority in their planning and transportation policy. Almost all forms of transport cater for the disabled as do many of the hotels, especially those which are part of the international chains. The Singaporeans themselves are also invariably helpful.

Access Singapore   Access Singapore is an access guide in English for people with disabilities published by the Singapore Council of Social Services and obtainable, either by post or to any visitor in person, from their information point for the disabled in Singapore (11 Penang Lane, Singapore 0923; tel. 336 15 44, 331 54 17).

## Drugs

In common with almost all Asian countries Singapore takes a very hard line on drugs, especially where drug-trafficking is concerned, and has tough penalties for possession – random searches are possible at any time – as well as for the importing, exporting and manufacture of drugs.

Penalties   The maximum penalty for using drugs is a 10-year prison sentence or S$20,000 fine, or both, while the death penalty is mandatory for anyone convicted of trafficking, manufacturing, importing or exporting controlled substances above a certain amount. This applies just as much to foreigners, and it is no good expecting any help from diplomatic quarters for these types of offences.

Beware of so-called "friends" asking you to take anything back on your homeward flight for them. There have been frequent attempts in the past to inveigle unsuspecting travellers into acting as drug couriers.

## Electricity

The voltage in Singapore is 220–240 volts 50 cycles per second. Hotels can usually provide visitors with adaptors or transformers if necessary.

## Emergency Services

| | |
|---|---|
| Tel. 999 | Police |
| Tel. 995 | Fire |
| Tel. 995 | Ambulance |
| AA road service (24 hours); tel. 748 99 11; fax: 733 50 94<br>AA Centre, River Valley Road | Breakdowns |
| See Health Care | Chemists |
| See Diplomatic Representation | Foreign missions |

## Events and Festivals

In a multi-cultural society like Singapore, where each of the ethnic communities has its own traditional festivals and religious celebrations, the year is packed with all kinds of colourful events. The dates vary from year to year since they are determined by different religious and lunar calendars so check for what's on in the daily press (see Newspapers and Periodicals) or with the Singapore Tourist Promotion Board.

Maulidin Nabi, commemorating the birth of the Prophet Mohammed     January
This festival falls on the twelfth day of the third month in the Muslim calendar. During religious ceremonies in all the mosques, to which visitors are welcome, Koranic scholars tell of the life and achievements of the Prophet in Arabic, English, Malay and Tamil. At about seven in the evening passages are read aloud from the "Berzanji", an account of the life of Mohammed. These ceremonies are at their most impressive in the Sultan Mosque (see A–Z, Sultan Mosque).

Thaipusam, Hindu procession of penitents
Hindu festival when penitents process between temples carrying decorated steel arches with skewers, spikes and hooks piercing their faces and bodies, to the accompaniment of drumming, dancing and chanting. Their route takes them from the Sri Srinivasa Perumal Temple (see A–Z) in Serangoon Road, via Selegie Road, Dhoby Gaut, Orchard Road and Clemenceau Avenue to Chettiar's Temple (see A–Z), returning in the evening by way of Maxwell Road, Robinson Road, Market Street, Cecil Street, Cross Street, New Bridge Street and River Valley Road.

Chinese New Year     February
In the weeks preceding the Chinese New Year the people of Chinatown spring-clean their homes and decorate them with red banners bearing good luck slogans as a prelude to the festivities ushering in the new lunar year early in February.
    Chingay 23 marks the Chinese New Year with a spectacular street procession along Orchard Road from Ngee Ann City to Dhoby Gaut, complete with lion dancers, dragons, stiltwalkers and decorative floats.

**Events and Festivals**

 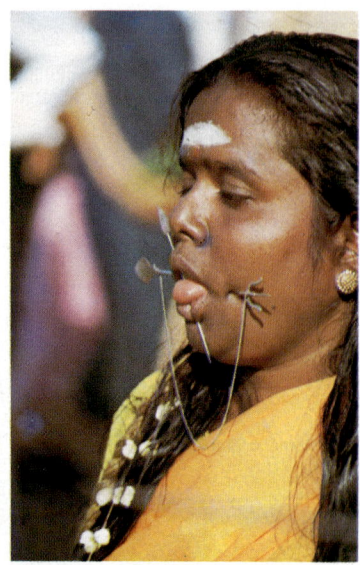

*Mortification of the flesh at the Thaipusam Festival*

March	Hari Raya Puasa, Muslim holiday following Ramadan
When the first day of the tenth lunar month in the Muslim calendar signals the end of the fasting month of Ramadan, believers gather in the mosques to pray, visit friends and relations, and celebrate with a festive meal. During the weeks before and after this grandest of all the Malay festivals Singapore's Malay area of Geylang is specially decorated and illuminated.

Birthday of the Monkey God
Celebrated twice a year – usually March and September – the birthday of this famous Chinese mythological character is marked by Chinese street opera and puppet plays in temple courtyards and processions of mediums who pierce their cheeks and tongues with long needles and hand out paper charms. These processions are particularly impressive in the temples on Eng Hoon and Cumming Street and, in September, the Monkey God Temple in Seng Poh Road.

April	Good Friday: Biennial International Film Festival (1995)

Songkhran Festival
This water festival is celebrated in the Thai buddhist temples in Silat and Holland Road, when images of Buddha are bathed and worshippers sprinkled with holy water to celebrate the new year.

May	Birthday of the Third Prince
The birthday of the third prince is a Taoist festival, celebrated twice a year in May and September, when the Third Prince of the Lotus is honoured as a hero and miracle-worker. According to legend this Chinese child god rides on "wheels of wind and fire" wearing a magic bracelet and carrying a spear. During the festival spirit mediums mortify their flesh and there is a street procession on North Boat Quay and celebrations at various Taoist temples.

# Events and Festivals

Vesak Day
This Buddhist festival celebrates the birth, enlightenment and entry into Nirvana of the Buddha. Believers flock to the temples to pray, monks in their saffron robes chant sutras throughout the day, the poor are given food and caged birds are freed to win merit for the devout. At many temples candlelight processions and performances of traditional dramas mark the end of the celebrations, which can be witnessed at all Singapore's Buddhist temples but are at their most impressive in the Temple of a Thousand Lights (see A–Z).

Hari Raya Haji, in honour of those who have made the pilgrimage to Mecca. This Muslim festival on the tenth day of the 12th month of the Muslim calendar and celebrated in most mosques, including the Sultan Mosque (see A–Z), is marked by a day of prayer when animals are ritually slaughtered and the meat distributed to the poor. The haji (hajiah for women) wear a white cap signifying that they have made the pilgrimage to Mecca.

Biennial Festival of Asian Peforming Arts (1995)
Dragon Boat Festival, fifth day of the fifth moon    June
The dragon boat festival commemorates Qu Yuan, an ancient Chinese poet-hero, who drowned himself in protest against injustice and corruption. "Chung", the special rice dumplings on sale in Chinatown (see A–Z), stuffed with meat and wrapped in bamboo leaves which are eaten during the festival or given to friends and relations, are said to recall the rice-balls thrown into the water to prevent the fish from devouring the great man.

Photo and Video Fair, World Trade Centre    July

Festival of the Hungry Ghosts, seventh month of the lunar year    July/August
During the seventh month of the lunar year the spirits of the dead are believed to return and wander abroad, so joss sticks are lit in front of Chinese homes and they are presented with offerings of food and mock

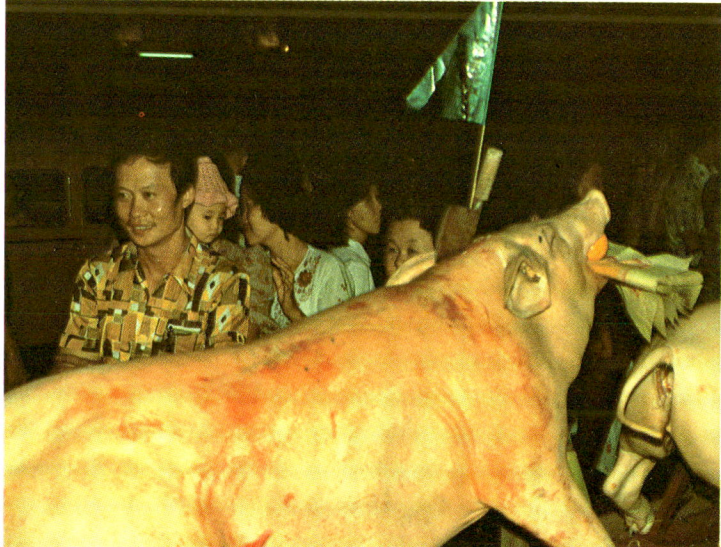

*Festival of the Hungry Ghosts*

**Events and Festivals**

money to appease them, while Chinese street opera and puppet plays are put on for their entertainment.

During the seventh month stall-holders in the city's markets provide lavish banquets and street opera. Spectators who give money are rewarded with fruit in return.

August — National Day (9 August)
The anniversary of the day when Singapore gained independence in 1965 is celebrated with a grand parade complete with dragon and lion dances and culminating in laser and firework displays.

September — Mooncake Festival, 15th day of the eighth month
The mooncake festival, celebrated on the night of the year when the moon is supposed to be at its fullest and brightest, is associated with the mooncakes on sale throughout Chinatown and filled with sweet bean paste, lotus seeds and duck-egg yolk. These are supposed to have carried messages between the 14th c. Chinese patriot Zhu Yan Zhang and his fellow rebels during their struggle to overthrow the tyrannical Mongol dynasty. This is also the time when in the Chinese Garden and elsewhere Chinese of all ages display their most colourful lanterns.

Birthday of the Monkey God. See March.

September/October — Navarathri, a festival celebrated in all Hindu temples
Navarathiri, meaning "nine nights" in Tamil, is dedicated to the consorts of the three gods in the Hindu trinity, namely Shiva the Destroyer, Vishnu the Protector, and Brahma, the Creator, with the first three days dedicated to Shiva's consort Parvathi, the second three to Lakshmi, goddess of wealth and consort of Vishnu, and the final three to Saraswathi, consort of Brahma.

Every night of the festival there are performances of classical Indian dance and music in the temples – especially Chettiar's Hindu Temple (see

*Moon Cake Festival*

## Events and Festivals

A–Z) – from around 7.30 to 10pm, with the final highlight on the tenth day a dramatic procession featuring a silver horse which starts out from Chettiar's Temple and makes its way along River Valley Road, Kelliney Road, Orchard Road and Clemenceau Avenue and back to the temple.

Thimithi, annual fire-walking ceremony in honour of Draupadi     October
Hindu devotees honour the goddess Draupadi, heroine of the Mahabharata, by processing from around 2pm from the Perumal Temple in Serangoon Road (see A–Z, Sri Srinivasa Temple) along Selegie Road, Prinsep Street, Bras Basah Road and North Bridge Road, ending up at the Sri Mariamman Temple (see A–Z) at around 5pm where the fire-walking takes place.

Deepavali, Hindu Festival of Lights
This important Indian holiday celebrates the triumph of light over darkness, of good over evil, when lamps are lit in Hindu homes and people dressed in their best visit their friends and relations. The streets in Little India and Hindu temples are festooned with lights and garlands and the shrines piled high with offerings.

Festival of the Nine Emperor Gods, ninth day of the ninth lunar month
During the nine days of this Chinese festival honouring the nine emperor gods, believed to cure ailments and bring long life and good fortune, there are performances of Chinese street opera and evening processions followed by crowds of people carrying yellow flags, to the accompaniment of cymbals and drums, as the images of the gods are paraded in decorative sedan chairs, each carried by eight men. The celebrations at the Kiu Ong Yiah Temple on Upper Serangoon Road and in Lorong Tai Seng are particularly impressive.

Pilgrimage to Kusu Island, ninth lunar month      October/
Throughout the lunar month some 100,000 Taoist pilgrims take brightly-     November
decorated boats to Kusu (Turtle) Island (see A–Z), where they light joss-

*Festival of the Nine Emperor Gods*

**Ferries**

| | |
|---|---|
| | sticks and candles in Tua Pekong Temple and pray for prosperity, good luck and well-behaved children. Both Chinese and Malays take part and visitors can watch by taking the ferry which leaves from Singapore Cruise Centre. |
| | Home Pride Asia, New Homes Exhibition, World Trade Centre |
| December | Christmas, with Christmas lights and decorated buildings from November to the beginning of January |
| Public Holidays | See entry |

## Ferries

| | |
|---|---|
| | Ferries to the islands around Singapore run at irregular intervals from Clifford Pier, Jardine Steps and the Singapore Cruise Centre at the World Trade Centre. |
| Northern islands | Departure from Ponggol Boatel (fast launches carrying 5 passengers); information: tel. 481 00 31/2; water skiing facilities. |
| Southern islands | Kusu Island, St. John's Islands: see A–Z |
| Pulau Hantu | See A–Z; charter boats from Jardine Steps or Clifford Pier. |
| Sentosa Island | See A–Z and Practical Information, Sightseeing. |
| Tanjong Pinang | Departure from Finger Pier daily, every two hours from 8.15am to 4.15 pm |
| Tanjong Belungkore | Ferrylink service from Changi Point, departing at 9am, noon and 4.15pm. Duration 45 minutes. Check in an hour before sailing. |
| Tioman Island | Daily except Wednesday at 7.50am from World Trade Centre. Duration 4½ hours. Check in at 6.30am. |

## Festivals

See Events and Festivals

## Folklore

| | |
|---|---|
| | Despite the rapid pace of modernisation and adoption of Western ways so evident in Singapore the folklore of the different ethnic groups in this multi-cultural society is still kept very much alive, as can be seen from the entry on Events and Festivals. More detailed information about traditional folklore presentations and events can be obtained from the Singapore Tourist Promotion Board (see Information). |
| Multi-cultural performances | The performances of Chinese, Malay and Indian song, dance and drama which take place throughout the year are listed in the what's on columns of the daily press and in the information supplied by the Singapore Tourist Board (see Information). |
| Chinese Opera | See entry |

## Food and Drink

| | |
|---|---|
| Eating with chopsticks | Most meals in East Asia are eaten with chopsticks, and Europeans will find it a good idea to try and use them as well. You will soon find the necessary |

**Food and Drink**

*Peking Duck, a Singapore delicacy*

manual dexterity comes with practice, and surprising as it may seem food actually tastes different if you use them. The reason for this is quite simple. With a fork you usually scoop up quite large mouthfuls and consequently the various ingredients in a dish all get eaten together. With chopsticks you only pick up a small amount at a time and thus get to savour every morsel on its own. And the fact that those preparing Chinese food also take particular care to retain and even intensify the special nature of each ingredient helps to heighten this effect.

Chopsticks come in a variety of materials ranging from plain bamboo to those which have been ornately lacquered or carved out of ivory. Hold the chopsticks in your right hand, with the lower one acting as a support, lying in the hollow between the thumb and the forefinger and resting on the tip of the "ring" finger; the upper one is 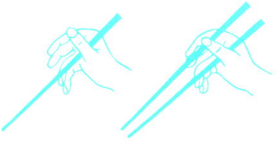 held between the thumb, forefinger and middle finger, and acts as a guide.

The Singaporeans claim to offer the greatest feast in the East. Their food certainly reflects the ethnic diversity of their population but above all provides an opportunity to sample the full range of Chinese cuisine, offering as it does specialities from all the different provinces such as Chiu Chow, Shanghai, Peking, and Szechuan, but the most popular of them all is Canton, where many of the country's Chinese community originally hail from, and most of the food sold by the hawkers and in many of the restaurants is Cantonese. On the whole Chinese food also tends to be cheaper.

Food

**Food and Drink**

Food stall ... ... and specialities

To enjoy the whole range of Eastern cuisine offered by Singapore try getting away from the big names and luxury hotels and venture out into the nearby streets. Public health standards are so high in Singapore that it is perfectly safe to eat food from even the smallest of stalls in a hawker centre, and the same goes for the city's many restaurants, although Western visitors sampling hot and spicy food for the first time should exercise the usual caution.

Dim Sum

Dim sum are the famous little Cantonese breakfast and lunchtime snacks, served on a tray or trolley from which you take your pick. They can be hot or cold and are mostly considered equally delicious whether your taste is Asian or European. Firm favourites include spring rolls (chun gun), shrimp miniature dumplings (ha gau) and sweet pork dumplings (siu mai).

Cantonese

The staple foods in Cantonese cooking, known for its lightness of touch, are rice, chicken, pork, fish and seafood. Dishes tend to be liquid-based rather than dry, sometimes containing ingredients unfamiliar to many European palates, but always freshly prepared. Although some diners may balk at ducks' feet or sea cucumbers there is certainly nothing untoward about such Cantonese classics as roast suckling pig or crisp deep-fried chicken. The usual accompaniment is rice, boiled or fried, with soya sauce, vinegar and chili sauce as condiments, and soup as the final course.

Chiu Chow

Chiu Chow specialities include braised goose, shark's fin soup thickened with chicken broth, soya sauce and ginger, steamed pig's trotters, and fried oysters in scrambled egg.

Peking

Restaurants specialising in Peking food are fewer than those for Cantonese food. Dishes from this northern province are spicier and more filling and tend to be accompanied by noodles rather than rice.

The best-known of them all is Peking duck, a real delicacy, especially the crispy roast skin. The meat is wrapped with spring onions and a special soya bean paste in thin "bao bing" pancakes. As a dish this is very filling and it usually needs to be ordered for four persons at a time in advance. The same applies to "beggar's chicken" which is delicately stuffed chicken, wrapped in lotus leaves and baked in a clay mould in hot ashes. Cracking open the clay with a hammer is quite a ceremony in itself.

Other typical Northern dishes include fish in wine sauce, mussels in chili sauce, fried bamboo shoots with green vegetables and "ziao zi", little ravioli-like pasta parcels filled with steamed or fried fish.

Teochow, or Mongolian hotpot, is a particular favourite in the winter months. This is made fondu-style in a chafing dish in the middle of the table, filled with well-seasoned hot broth, in which slivers of raw meat, vegetables or fish are boiled rapidly before the broth is consumed.

**Shanghai**

Shanghai dishes, which are even spicier than those from Peking, include fried eel with soya sauce, shrimps with green peas, meat balls with vegetables, sliced beef with green chili and fried crab.

**Szechuan**

The Szechuan style of cooking is also gaining in popularity among those who like their food highly spiced. Specialities include shredded pork in garlic sauce, sweet and sour fish, fried spicy shrimp, and marinated duck.

**Western food**

The chefs in all the big hotels are well up to standard so far as European and international fare is concerned.

**Desserts**

Desserts worth trying are "mai tai go" (water chestnuts) and "sai mai bo din" (sweet rice pudding).

**Fruit**

South-east Asia is a veritable orchard of exotic fruits, many of them virtually unknown in the West, and fresh fruit can be found in most of the restaurants depending on the season. If you eat fruit bought from a market remember to wash it thoroughly first.

Fresh pineapple is in season from April to July and comes in several varieties. Low in calories and high in vitamin C, it is sometimes eaten after fermentation but this can have a laxative effect.

Bananas are harvested all year round. When served as a dessert they are usually steeped in sweet coconut milk then grilled. Remember, the smaller the banana, the sweeter the taste.

Durian, which is in season from April to June, is a rather fleshy fruit prized as a delicacy by the locals but colloquially known as "stink fruit" by Europeans because of its smell, which is why most hotels prefer their guests not to bring it in.

Jack-fruit, heavy round fruits weighing several pounds, are sweet and aromatic and in season from August to September. They are usually served sliced on a bed of ice.

Coconuts provide a refreshing healthy drink with their milk, while the flesh is eaten out of the shell with a pointed spoon.

The local lemons are green and round and available throughout the year. The yellow lemons familiar to Europeans are imported and very expensive.

Lychees, with delicious succulent white flesh in a hard red skin, are in season from May to August. Another fruit very similar to the lychee is the rambutan.

Next to pineapple the tourist's favourite is undoubtedly mango, in season from March to June. These are only sweet and juicy when yellow-skinned and fully ripe. Cut them in half and then spoon or suck out the flesh.

**Getting to Singapore**

*Mouthwatering fruit*

Oranges, available here all year round, have thin green skins. The yellow ones are particularly sweet.

Grapefruits, also in season throughout the year, usually are the delicious pink-fleshed variety which tastes even better with a pinch of salt.

The cheapest of all the Asian fruits is papaya, found on market stalls throughout the year and served at hotel breakfasts in halves with a slice of lemon. Just remember that papaya eaten in large quantities definitely acts as a laxative.

The rose-apple (January–March) tends to resemble a pear, with a rust-coloured skin and soft white flesh, both of which can be eaten. Since it has a rather sharp taste it is best eaten with sugar and a pinch of salt.

Drink

Singapore's water supply is drinkable but highly chlorinated. Most Chinese drink nothing but tea with their meals. Another local favourite is "buah susu", a rather sharp-tasting, milky-white drink made from passion fruit. When it comes to alcoholic drinks the Singaporeans prefer beer, whisky, brandy or rice-wine (shao xing or mao tai). This is usually drunk warm and the best-known brand is "Hua Diao", although "Jia Fan", which is cheaper, is considered better. You can get virtually every imaginable brand of beer and spirits in Singapore, but the Chinese beer from Tsingtau on the mainland is considerably cheaper.

Restaurants

See entry

## Getting to Singapore

By air

Visitors to Singapore usually travel by air and fly into its ultra-modern international airport at Changi, served by scheduled flights from most English-speaking capitals (see Air Travel).

For travellers coming from Malaysia there are several shuttle flights between Kuala Lumpur and Singapore daily. The fares are considerably cheaper and passengers without seat reservations are dealt with on a first come, first served basis.

Singapore is on Asian Highway A1 from London to Vietnam but since it is currently not possible to drive through Myanmar (Burma) the only access by road is from Malaysia. The drive from Kuala Lumpur can take as little as six hours and is on an excellent motorway, with its final stretch over the Singapore-Johore causeway. There are also scheduled daily coach services along the same route. These take about seven hours including a short stopover for meals and refreshments (see Bus Trips).

By road

Singapore is part of the rail network of Peninsular Malaysia and there are several air-conditioned express services a day, including overnight sleepers, from Kuala Lumpur (see Rail Travel). A relatively recent introduction is the weekly Eastern and Orient Express, the de luxe train service which departs from Bangkok every Wednesday and runs down through Malaysia into Singapore. For information contact Eastern and Orient Express Co., tel. 227 20 68, fax 224 92 65 (Singapore) or the nearest Singapore Tourist Promotion Board office (see Information).

By rail

Like many other ports in south-east Asia Singapore is a destination for cruise ships such as the Canberra, Sea Princess, Sagafjord and QE2, and some cargo ships with passenger accommodation, including those sailing several times a month from Antwerp, Rotterdam and Hamburg. For further information contact your travel agent. There are also several passenger boats a week between Singapore and Malaysia (see Boat Cruises, Ferries).

By sea

## Golf

See Sport

## Health Care

Any holiday in the tropics requires a certain amount of advance preparation to ensure you enjoy the experience to the full, so consult your doctor or local travel clinic beforehand to check on any health risks, especially if you are pregnant or taking young children.

No vaccinations are necessary so far as the Singapore authorities are concerned unless you are coming from an area affected with cholera or yellow fever in which case vaccination certificates are required. However, you would be well advised to have up-to-date protection against polio and tetanus and carry your health passport with you, if you have one, together with notification of your bloodgroup and any possible allergies.

Vaccinations

It is also advisable to get protection against hepatitis A which can be transmitted through the unhygienic preparation of food and drink, especially ice.

Malaria has recently been on the increase in south-east Asia so it is advisable to take some form of prophylactic, especially if visits are planned away from the tourist mainstream. Consult your travel clinic for the most appropriate method.

Malaria

A travelling medical kit assumes greater importance in this part of the world because of the greater risk of infection and the possibility that many medicines available at home may be unobtainable or go under a different name. Needless to say it is advisable to take an adequate supply of any currently prescribed medication (see below, Chemists).

Medical kit

**Health Care**

Your medical kit should also include scissors, tweezers, cotton wool, bandages, plasters, antiseptic cream, disinfectant, painkillers and something for stomach upsets, travel sickness, etc., as well as insect repellant and sun-protection, together with cream or lotion for sunburn, bites and stings.

On the plane — For the long flight wear light, comfortable clothing and footwear – seasoned travellers actually prefer slippers – and try using an inflatable neck-support to help you sleep.

Acclimatisation — Your body takes time to get used to the tropical climate so avoid physical exertion for the first few days. Air-conditioning has its problems too, so carry a light wrap or jacket and avoid too much switching from hot to cold, i.e. as between outdoors and indoors. Also turn the air-conditioning down or even off at night so as not to get too cold.

Exposure to sun — Singapore is not far from the Equator so do not spend too much time out in the full sun, especially without some form of protection. High-factor barrier creams are essential.

Food — Since Singapore has very strict health controls it is generally safe to eat food from the hawker centres, but avoid anything uncooked, fruit which has not been peeled, icecream, and drinks with ice in them, and always wash fruit thoroughly before eating.

Aids — Take all the well-known precautionary measures against HIV and Aids, and take your own needles if you have to have injections; be aware of the dangers involved in blood transfusions, surgery and dental treatment.

## Medical Facilities

The Singaporeans believe that their medical facilities are among the finest in the world. Most hotels also have their own doctor on 24-hour call, and they can be contacted if required through the front desk or room service.

Doctors are listed in the Yellow Pages under "Medical Practitioners", and dentists under "Dental Surgeons".

There is no free health care for visitors so it is advisable to take out some form of insurance to cover medical costs, especially since you will be expected to pay straightaway. Many hospitals may also require an advance down-payment on the final cost of treatment.

Emergency number — In a medical emergency call 995.

## Hospitals

Alexandra Hospital
Alexandra Road; tel. 63 52 52

Mount Elizabeth Hospital; tel. 737 26 66

National University Hospital; tel. 779 55 55
(dialysis unit; tel. 259 92 17)

Singapore General Hospital
Outram Road; tel. 222 33 22

Tao Payoh Hospital
Tao Payoh Road; tel. 256 04 11

## Chemists and Pharmacies

Pharmacies, as chemists are known in Singapore, are to be found in nearly every shopping centre. For names and addresses look under "Pharmacies" in the Yellow Pages. Most medication is only dispensed on a doctor's prescription, and if you are on any special medication it is advisable to take a supply from home since if it is available it may be sold under a different name. It is also worth noting that anyone taking in medicines which may only be obtained by prescription under Singapore law, especially sleeping pills, depressants and stimulants, must have a doctor's prescription confirming that they are for personal use while travelling.

In an emergency call 995. — Emergency number

Registered pharmacies are open from 9am to 6pm, with some shops staying open until 10pm. — Opening times

# Hotels

Singapore's hotels rank among the best in the world by international standards and for many of them it is advisable to book well ahead, especially if the proposed visit coincides with holidays such as Christmas or the Chinese New Year.

Hotel reservations made abroad should be confirmed on arrival at the hotel desk in Changi Airport. This is also the best place to find a hotel room if it has not been booked in advance. — Reservations

Hotels usually add a 10% service charge. There is also a goods and service tax (GST) of 3% on most goods and services but this can be refundable for visitors so check with the STPB leaflet "Tax Refund for Visitors to Singapore". — Tax and service charge

The hotels listed below, which are only a small selection, are in alphabetical order and in three broad categories according to price range. Generally speaking the room rates for these categories are as follows, but they can vary considerably outside this range and should be checked against the "Guide to Hotels" published by the Singapore Tourist Promotion Board: — Classification

Luxury/top range: single room S$150–280, double S$200 plus
Middle range: single room S$60–100, double S$80–130
Budget: single room S$30–60, double S$50–80

Allson Hotel, 101 Victoria Street; tel. 336 08 11 — Luxury/top range
Amara Hotel, 165 Tanjong Pagar; tel. 224 44 88
Ana Hotel, 16 Nassim Hill; tel. 732 12 22
Apollo Hotel, 405 Havelock Road; tel. 733 20 81
Bayview Inn, 30 Bencoolen Street; tel. 337 28 82
Beaufort, Singapore, Sentosa Island; tel. 275 03 31
Boulevard Hotel, 200 Orchard Boulevard; tel. 737 29 11
Cairnhill Hotel, 19 Cairnhill Circle; tel. 734 66 22
Carlton Hotel, 76 Bras Basah Road; tel. 338 83 33
Cockpit Hotel, 6/7 Oxley Rise; tel. 737 91 11
Crown Prince Hotel, 270 Orchard Road; tel. 732 11 11
★Dynasty Hotel, 320 Orchard Road; tel. 734 99 00
Excelsior Hotel, 5 Coleman Street; tel. 338 77 33
Furama Hotel, 60 Eu Tong Sen Street; tel. 533 38 88
Garden Hotel, 14 Balmoral Road; tel. 235 33 44
Golden Landmark Hotel, 390 Victoria Street; tel. 297 28 28
★Goodwood Park Hotel, 22 Scotts Road; tel. 737 74 11
Harbour View Dai-Ichi, 81 Anson Road; tel. 224 11 33
★Hilton International, 581 Orchard Road; tel. 737 22 33
★Holiday Inn Park View, 11 Cavenagh Road; tel. 733 83 33
Hotel Asia, 37 Scotts Road; tel. 737 83 88

**Hotels**

*Inn of the 6th Happiness*

Hotel Equatorial, 429 Bukit Timah Road; tel. 732 04 31
Hotel Grand Central, 22 Cavenagh Road; tel. 737 99 44
Hotel Imperial, 1 Jalan Rumbia; tel. 737 16 66
★Hyatt Regency, 10/12 Scotts Road; tel. 738 12 34
★Inn of Sixth Happiness, 9/37 Erskine Road; tel. 223 32 66
★King's Hotel Clarion, Havelock Road; tel. 733 00 11
Ladyhill Hotel, 1 Ladyhill Road; tel. 737 21 11
Le Meridien Changi, 1 Netheravon Road; tel. 542 77 00
Le Meridien Singapore, 100 Orchard Road; tel. 733 88 55
★Mandarin Singapore, 333 Orchard Road; tel. 737 44 11
★Marina Mandarin Singapore, 6 Raffles Boulevard; tel. 338 33 88
Melia At Scotts, 45 Scotts Road; tel. 732 58 85
★New Otani Singapore, 177A River Valley Road; tel. 338 33 33
New Park Hotel, 181 Kitchener Road; tel. 291 55 33
Novotel Orchid, 214 Dunearn Road; tel. 250 33 22
Omni Marco Polo, 247 Tanglin Road; tel. 474 71 41
★Orchard Hotel, 442 Orchard Road; tel. 734 77 66
Orchard Parade Hotel, 1 Tanglin Road; tel. 737 11 33
★Oriental Singapore, Marina Square, 5 Raffles Avenue; tel. 338 00 66
★Pan Pacific Hotel, Marina Square, 7 Raffles Boulevard; tel. 336 81 11
Phoenix Hotel, 277 Orchard Road; tel. 737 86 66
Plaza Hotel, 7500A Beach Road; tel. 298 00 11
★Raffles Hotel, 1 Beach Road; tel. 337 18 86 (see A–Z, Raffles Hotel)
★Regent of Singapore, 1 Cuscaden Road; tel. 733 88 88
★Shangri-La-Hotel, 22 Orange Grove Road; tel. 737 36 44
Sheraton Towers, 39 Scotts Road; tel. 737 68 88
Singapore Paramount Hotel, 25 Marine Parade Road; tel. 344 55 77
Singapore Peninsula, 3 Coleman Street; tel. 337 22 00
★Westin Stamford, 2 Stamford Road; tel. 338 85 85 (world's tallest hotel!)

Middle range

Bencoolen, 47 Bencoolen Street; tel. 336 08 22
Broadway, 195 Serangoon Road; tel. 292 46 61

Katong Park Hotel, 42/46 Meyer Road; tel. 345 33 11
★Lion City, 15 Tanjong Katong Road; tel. 744 81 11
Premier, 22 Nassim Hill; tel. 733 98 11
RELC International House, 30 Orange Grove Road; tel. 737 90 44
Seaview, 26 Amber Close; tel. 345 22 22

Singapore has many other hotels with more modest facilities but a high standard of cleanliness. The Singapore Tourist Promotion Board (see Information) also keeps a list of approximately 40 budget hotels. Budget

Majestic, 31/37 Bukit Pasoh Road; tel. 222 33 77
New Mayfair, 40/44 Armenian Street; tel. 337 45 42
Metropolitan YMCA, 60 Stevens Road; tel. 737 77 55
Ria Country Club, 447A Upper East Coast Road; tel. 41 02 22
Station Hotel, Station Building, Keppel Road; tel. 222 15 51/3

See entry Youth Hostels

# Information

## Singapore Tourist Promotion Board

The Singapore Tourist Promotion Board (STPB) is the Government tourist authority, and represents the interests of the country's tourist industry abroad as well being responsible for tourism within Singapore. Visitors can go to the STPB not only for information and its excellent publications but also if they feel they have been overcharged or treated discourteously. Any complaints are then passed on to Singapore's Consumer Association (Trade Union House Annexe, Shenton Way; tel. 222 41 65).

STPB Head Office: #36–04 Raffles City Tower, 250 North Bridge Road, Singapore 0617; tel. 339 66 22, fax 339 94 23

#02–34 Raffles Hotel Arcade, 328 North Bridge Road;
tel. 1–800–334 13 35/6
Open: 8.30am–6pm; MRT station City Hall Tourist Information Centres

#02/03 Scotts Shopping Centre, 6 Scotts Road; tel. 738 37 78/9
Open: 9.30am–9.30pm; MRT station Orchard Road

STPB publications include the "Singapore Weekly Guide" as well as an official guide for each month. "Singapore Weekly Guide"

For assistance with conferences apply to the Singapore Convention Bureau (tel. 339 66 22). Conferences

Information on trade fairs and exhibitions is available from the STPB (tel. 339 66 22), or the World Trade Centre (tel. 271 22 11). Trade fairs and exhibitions

Malaysia Tourism Promotion Board
G 3, Ocean Building, Collyer Quay; tel. 532 63 51 Excursions to Malaysia

Indonesia Tourist Promotion Office,
Ocean Building, 10 Collyer Quay; tel. 534 28 37 Excursions to Indonesia

## STPB Offices Abroad

8th Floor, St. Georges Court,
16 St George's Terrace, Perth WA 6000
tel. (09) 325 85 78, fax (09) 221 38 64 Australia

## Insurance

|  | Suite 1202, Level 12, Westpac Plaza,<br>60 Margaret Street, Sydney NSW 2000<br>tel. (02) 241 37 71, fax (02) 252 35 86 |
|---|---|
| Canada | The Standard Life Centre, 121 King Street West,<br>Suite 1000, Toronto, Ontario M5H 3T9<br>tel. (416) 363 88 98, fax (416) 363 57 52 |
| New Zealand | c/o General Travel Marketing Ltd., Dataset House,<br>143 Nelson Street, Auckland<br>tel. (09) 358 11 91, fax (09) 358 11 96 |
| United Kingdom | 1st Floor, Carrington House,<br>126/130 Regent Street, London W1R 5FE<br>tel. (0171) 437 00 33, fax (0171) 734 21 91 |
| United States<br>of America | 2 Prudential Plaza, 180 North Stetson Avenue,<br>Suite 1450, Chicago, Illinois 60601<br>tel. (312) 938 18 88, fax (312) 938 00 86 |
|  | 8484 Wilshire Boulevard, Suite 510,<br>Beverly Hills, Los Angeles, CA 90211<br>tel. (213) 852 19 01, fax (213) 852 01 29 |
|  | 590 Fifth Avenue, 12th Floor,<br>New York, NY 10036<br>tel. (212) 302 48 61, fax (212) 302 48 01 |

## Insurance

| | |
|---|---|
| General | Visitors are strongly advised to ensure that they have adequate holiday insurance to cover the main risks involved in a journey to Asia, including loss or damage to luggage, loss of currency and valuables. This is usually included with an organised package holiday. |
| Medical Insurance | See Health Care |

## Language

See Facts and Figures, Language

## Libraries and Archives

| | |
|---|---|
| Libraries | The National Library of Singapore in Stamford Road has a stock of over 2.7 million titles – 310,000 in Malay, 740,000 in Chinese, 86,200 in Tamil and 1.5 million in English.<br>It also has large collections of microfilms, recordings and photographs, all of which are open to the public, as well as a special section of books for the blind. Opening hours are 8.30am to 8pm Monday to Friday.<br><br>The University Library System carries over 700,000 books, 6000 periodicals, 25,000 microfilm titles and an international selection of newspapers. |
| Archives | The National Archives, established in 1968, hold documents on the history of Singapore dating back to 1805. Records are available for consultation by the public provided they are over 25 years old. The archives also hold records on microfilm from private collections. |

The Ministry of Culture also runs an oral history unit containing recordings of personal accounts relating to the history of Singapore. Subjects already covered include pioneers of Singapore, and political development between 1945 and 1965, while a project is under way on the aftermath of the Japanese Occupation.

## Lost Property

There is a "lost and found" office at Changi Airport where found items are brought for safe keeping. For anything that may have been left in a bus or taxi contact the Registry of Vehicles (ROV, Sin Ming Drive; tel. 459 42 22). It is also advisable to report any loss to the police.

## Markets

See A–Z

## Measurements

Singapore uses the metric system for weights and measures but temperature is usually recorded in Fahrenheit.

## Motoring

| | |
|---|---|
| The only road access to Singapore is from Malaysia over the Johore causeway. Once on the island there is a good network of roads and expressways, but these can get very crowded. | Roads |
| The rule of the road is drive on the left and overtake on the right. Speed limits are 50kph/30mph in built-up areas, 70kph/40mph elsewhere, and 80kph/50mph on expressways. Traffic is very well-disciplined and rigorously supervised by the police. Drinking and driving is also subject to heavy penalties. To prevent congestion a permit is needed during the morning and evening rush-hours for cars with fewer than four people wanting to drive in the Central Business District. | Driving in Singapore |
| Foreign drivers no longer require an international driving licence provided they can produce their own national one. | Driving licence |
| Pedestrians may only cross the road on designated crossings, and anyone caught jaywalking is liable to a fine. | Pedestrians |
| In the event of an accident or breakdown in a hire car it is advisable to notify the company concerned. For information and assistance you can also turn to the Automobile Association of Singapore which operates a 24-hour road service (tel. 748 99 11). The AA address is: | Accidents/ breakdowns |

Automobile Association of Singapore (AA),
336 River Valley Road, Singapore 0409; tel. 737 24 44

| | |
|---|---|
| Anyone bringing their own car into Singapore for up to 12 months requires a carnet de passage (the speed limit on motorways in Malaysia is 110kph/68mph). See also Getting to Singapore. | Driving to Singapore |

## Museums

National Museum, see A–Z
Changi Prison Chapel and Museum, Upper Changi Road North;
    tel. 743 78 85. Open: Mon.–Sat. 9.30am–4.30pm. Free admission.

Chinaman Scholar's Gallery, 14B Trengganu Street; tel. 222 95 54. Open: Mon.–Sat. 9am–4pm.
Empress Place Museum, Empress Place Building; tel. 336 76 33
Mint Coin Gallery, 249 Jalan Boon Lay; tel. 261 47 49. Open: Mon.–Fri. 9am–4pm. Admission free.
Peranakan Place Museum, 180 Orchard Road, Peranakan Place; tel. 732 69 66. Open: Mon.–Fri. 10.30am–3.30pm.
Singapore Air Force Museum, Blk 78 Cranwell Road, off Loyang Avenue; tel. 540 15 37. Open: Tue.–Sun. 10am–4.30pm. Admission free.
Royal Selangor Pewter Museum, 32 Pandan Road; tel. 265 77 11. Open: 9am–5.30pm daily. Admission free.

## Newspapers and Periodicals

Local press

Singapore has three daily papers in English, "The Straits Times", founded in 1845, "Business Times", and an evening tabloid, "The New Paper", plus several other Chinese, Malay and Indian dailies. "The Straits Times" is noted for its full and excellent coverage of international news.

International press

Hotels and the larger news stands carry a number of British and other European dailies, as well as the "International Herald Tribune" which is edited in Paris and published the same day in Singapore.

Press imports

See Customs Regulations

## Nightlife

Singapore's nightlife is relatively sedate compared with other oriental cities such as Bangkok and Hong Kong, although recent years have seen quite a boom in new discos, bars and nightclubs. This is probably a sign of Singapore's growing prosperity, especially among the young, but everywhere tends to be expensive whoever the clientele.

Bars and pubs

Bars and pubs with live music, especially jazz and blues, are becoming increasingly popular. These include the Saxophone Bar (23 Cuppage Terrace), Anywhere (Tanglin Shopping Centre), Somerset's Bar (Westin Stamford Hotel), and Bill Bailey's (Dynasty Hotel), to name but a few.

Cocktail lounges

Hotel cocktail lounges often have a piano, guitar, or small orchestra providing the background music.

Discos

Discos abound in the city and most of the top hotels. Particular favourites with the young include The Warehouse (332 Havelock Road), Kasbah (in the Mandarin Hotel, complete with Arabian decor), Top Ten (Claymore Drive) and Chameleon (Marine Village). For information ask the Singapore Tourist Promotion Board (see Information) or hotel reception.

Nightclubs

Nightclubs, some with midnight floorshows, tend to be in the big international hotels, where they can be very pricy indeed given the high-spending habits of the patrons.

Remember, whether nightclubbing or discoing, T-shirts and trainers are definitely out!

## Opening Times

Banks

Mon.–Fri. 9.30am–3pm, Sat. 9.30–11.30am

Money changers

Opening times vary depending on the location, but usually licensed money changers are open Mon.–Sat. 9/10am–7pm.

**Photography and Film**

| | |
|---|---|
| 9am–6pm (see Health Care) | Chemists |
| 10am–10pm daily, sometimes midnight. Several department stores close on Sundays. | Department stores |
| See Post | Post offices |
| 9am–10pm, sometimes midnight. Some shops have Sunday closing. | Shops |
| Mon.–Fri. 8am–5pm, Sat. 8am–1pm | Offices |

For Diplomatic Representation, Museums, see entries

## Parks and Nature Reserves

As an island state with no hinterland to speak of Singapore has gone to great pains to conserve its green-space, both in the city itself and the countryside round about. Its image as a garden city concerned to preserve its tropical flora and wildlife is well deserved. The city has many parks and gardens, with footpaths winding their way amid tropical plants and a colourful sea of flowers, while areas of primary rainforest have been protected as nature reserves.

Botanic Gardens, see A–Z
Bukit Timah Reserve, see A–Z
Central Park, see A–Z
Elizabeth Walk, see A–Z
Empress Place, see A–Z
Jurong, see A–Z
MacRitchie Reservoir, see A–Z
Mandai Orchid Gardens, see A–Z
Mount Faber, see A–Z
Padang, see A–Z
Seletar Reservoir, see A–Z
Sentosa Island, see A–Z

## Photography and Film

Singapore is packed with photo-opportunities and nowhere is out of bounds to the camera. Although most local people enjoy having their picture taken you should still always ask permission – a gesture with the camera will usually suffice – and accept any refusal gracefully. Some devout Hindus and Buddhists refuse to be photographed because of their beliefs, and it goes without saying that no-one should be approached at close quarters during their religious observances. Experienced photographers use a telephoto or zoom lens so that they can keep their distance.
The best time for photography is in the morning and when the sun is past its height in the afternoon. You will definitely need a filter, plus special lens-cleaning materials to guard against the ravages of salt in the air and water. Keep the lens covered when not in use.
Using religious objects as adjuncts for holiday snaps causes great offence and any climbing on temple walls or statues is strictly forbidden and carries a heavy fine. Hindus, for example, regard this as a desecration of their holy sites.
If you make a promise to send someone a copy of a photograph you must keep your word or otherwise lose face, which is the worst thing that can happen to anyone in Asian eyes.

| | |
|---|---|
| Singapore has plenty of good facilities for cheap and quick film-processing. | Developing |

**Post**

*Wedding photograph with a difference*

| | |
|---|---|
| Airport controls | Carry all film in your hand luggage since this can safely go through the airport scanners. If in doubt about particularly sensitive materials insist on having them checked by hand. |

## Post

| | |
|---|---|
| Post offices | Singapore has 66 post offices providing a full service and 56 sub post offices. Inner city local urgent mail posted at 24 specially designated post offices gets to its destination anywhere on the main island within 2½ hours.<br>Most hotels also provide postal services at the reception desk. |
| Head post office | General Post Office<br>Fullerton Building; tel. 533 02 34 |
| Opening times | The GPO and Comcentre branch are both open round the clock for basic postal services. Changi Airport Post Office is open from 8am to 8pm Monday to Saturday. |
| Stamps | Stamps are on sale at all post offices and from licensed stamp dealers. There are two societies for stamp collectors, the Singapore Philatelic Society (160 Cross Street), and the Singapore Stamp Club (28 Swattenham Road). |

## Public Holidays

New Year's Day (January 1)
Chinese New Year (two days)
Hari Raya Puasa
Good Friday

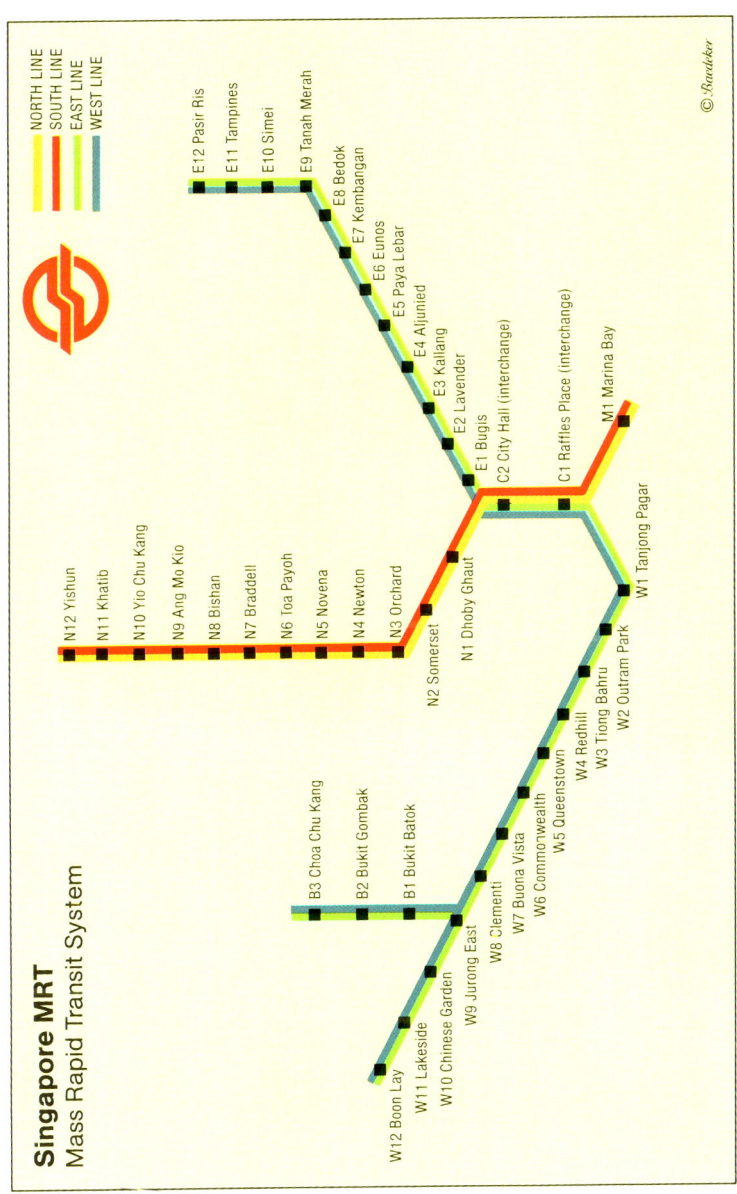

**Public Transport**

*Pleasing architecture: outside (Orchard MRT Station) . . .*

Labour Day (May 1)
Hari Raya Haji
Vesak Day
National Day (August 9)
Deepavali
Christmas Day (December 25)

See also Events and Festivals

# Public Transport

Buses
Singapore's buses, mostly operated by the Singapore Bus Service (SBS) and the Trans Island Bus Service (TIBS), run frequent and quite cheap services, usually from around 6am to midnight but depending on the day of the week and the line. The SBS also operates inner-city shuttle buses in the Central Business District (CBD)
 The TIBS lines mainly cover routes in the Sembawang and Woodlands areas, while the Blue Arrow service covers four express routes around the island. The airport bus service (No. 390) runs on three routes between the airport and all the big hotels.
 Fares are collected by the driver and it helps to have the exact fare ready. One way round this is to get a visitor's Singapore Explorer ticket (see Sightseeing) which is valid for one or three days.

Bus Guide
The Singapore Bus Guide and more detailed bus and MRT timetables can be obtained from travel agents, bookstores, newsagents and the Singapore Tourist Promotion Board.

Trolleys
There is also a Singapore Trolley bus service from 9am to 10pm between the Orchard Road area, Tanjong Pagar and the World Trade Centre (see Sightseeing).

**Radio and Television**

... and in (City Hall Station)

Singapore's Mass Rapid Transit System, which first opened in December 1987, has 41 stations (15 of them underground) and covers a network of 66km/41 miles. It was completed in a record time of seven years at a cost of S$5 billion and carries an estimated 800,000 people a day. The MRT extends from the city centre (Raffles Place) to the satellite town of Yishun in the north, Boon Lay in Jurong to the west and Pasir Ris to the east.

Trains run from 6am until midnight at intervals of between three and eight minutes. Fares to each destination are posted up at all stations.

MRT (Mass Rapid Transit System)

For the MRT route map see back inside cover.

MRT route map

Sentosa Island can be reached by the cable car which runs daily between 8.30am and 9pm from Mount Faber and the World Trade Centre.

Cable Car

Trishaws are less of a common sight than they used to be on the streets of Singapore but this traditional mode of travel by pedal power is still a good way to go sightseeing in, say, Chinatown (see Sightseeing). Agree on the price before embarking.

Trishaws

## Radio and Television

Singapore radio, which first began broadcasting in 1936, is predominantly in English but there are also some programmes in Chinese, Tamil, and Malay.

Radio

The country's first national television broadcast was in 1963 in black and white, with colour arriving in 1974. The Singapore Broadcasting Corporation is state-controlled, transmitting its largely English-speaking programmes on three channels. It is also possible to get the three Malaysian TV channels.

Television

Some hotels also have Pay-TV and their own in-house video programmes to promote events, special offers, etc.

**Rail Travel**

*Mount Faber Cable Car Station (to Sentosa Island)*

## Rail Travel

Singapore forms part of the Malaysian Railways network, with regular services to all places on Malaysia's west coast, Kuala Lumpur, Penang/Butterworth and the northern east coast, departing daily from its single railway station on Keppel Road (tel. 222 51 65).

The trains have 1st and 2nd class compartments, some with air-conditioning and overnight sleepers.

See also Getting to Singapore

## Religious Services

All places of worship are listed in the Yellow Pages under Church Services. Phone the numbers given below for times of services:

| | |
|---|---|
| Anglican | Saint Andrew's Cathedral, Saint Andrew's Road; tel. 337 61 04 |
| Baptist | Baptist Church, 90 King's Road; tel. 466 49 29 |
| Catholic | Cathedral of the Good Shepherd, Queen Street; tel. 337 68 70 |
| Jewish | Jewish Synagogue, Waterloo Street; tel. 336 06 92 |
| Lutheran | Queenstown Lutheran Church, 709 Commonwealth Drive; tel. 63 78 66 |
| Methodist | Wesley Church, 5 Fort Canning Road; tel. 336 14 33 |
| Presbyterian | Presbyterian Church, 3 Orchard Road; tel. 337 66 81 |
| Salvation Army | Salvation Army, 207 Clemenceau Avenue; tel. 737 91 22 |

# Restaurants

Singapore offers culinary delights from all over the world in its restaurants but its forte, and hence its claim to host the greatest feast in the East, is clearly the rich variety of Asian cuisine, especially Chinese.

As a general rule there is no need to reserve a table in advance except in the most exclusive restaurants. Once in a restaurant it is customary to wait until you can be shown to a table. Menus are always available in English.

Reservation

For an unusual setting try "breakfast with the birds" at Jurong's Bird Park (see A–Z, Jurong Town) or take tea with the animals in the Zoological Gardens (see A–Z).

Eating from hawker stalls very much reflects the Asian habit of snacking throughout the day rather than sitting down to a communal meal. In Singapore many of these stalls are brought together in hawker centres with each stall probably specialising in only one or two dishes, cooked while you wait. Very tasty they are too, often consisting of rice or noodles with chicken, pork or beef, and various kinds of seafood. This being Singapore there is no need to worry about health and safety since even the smallest stall is checked regularly by government health inspectors. Hawker stalls abound throughout the island but good places to find them are Newton Circus, the Lagoon Food Centre and Chinatown.

Hawker food

See entry

Tipping

The following list of restaurants is of necessity but a small selection among so many.

Listed entries

Cantonese (light and cleverly seasoned):

Chinese

Fook Yuen Seafood Restaurant
#03–05/08 Paragon Shopping Centre; tel. 235 22 11

Grand City Chinese Restaurant
#07–04 Cathay Building; tel. 338 36 22

House of Blossoms
Marina Mandarin Hotel, 6 Raffles Boulevard; tel. 338 33 88

House of Four Seasons
#01–03 Empress Place Building, 1 Empress Place; tel. 339 68 33

Inn of Happiness
Hilton International Singapore, 581 Orchard Road; tel. 737 22 33

Kirin Court Seafood & Shark's Fin Restaurant
20 Devonshire Road; tel. 732 11 88

Lei Garden
Boulevard Hotel, 200 Orchard Boulevard; tel. 235 81 22

Li Bai
Sheraton Hotel & Towers, 39 Scotts Road; tel. 737 68 88

Summer Palace
The Regent of Singapore, 1 Cuscaden Road; tel. 733 88 88

Tang Court
The Dynasty Singapore, 320 Orchard Road; tel. 734 99 00

Ru Yi Restaurant
Hyatt Regency Singapore, 10/12 Scotts Road; tel. 733 11 88

**Restaurants**

Tai Tong Hoi Kee
3 Mosque Street; tel. 223 34 84

Tsui Hang Village Restaurant
#02–142/145 Marina Square; tel. 338 66 68

Tung Lok Shark's Fin Restaurant
#04–07/09 Liang Court Complex, 177 River Valley Road
Tel. 336 60 22

Wah Lok Restaurant
Carlton Hotel, 76 Bras Basah Road; tel. 338 83 33

Yick Sang Restaurant
7 Ann Siang Hill; tel. 221 41 87

Hokkien — Good places to try Hokkien food, famous for its fish and seafood, are the hawker centres on Hokkien Street, Rasa Singapura, Newton Circus, and the Food Alley (Murray Street) in Beng Hiang.

Teochew — The following restaurants serve Teochew (Chinese fondu/Mongolian hotpot):

Feng Cheng Lou
270 Orchard Road

Chao Zhou
UIC Building, 5 Shenton Way

Hung Kang Restaurant
38 North Canal Road; tel. 533 53 00

Ban Sang Restaurant
New Bridge Road (specialities: grilled pork, roast duck)

Chui Wah Lin
Mosque Street (Teochew banquet)

Ng Mui Song Eating House
268 River Valley Road

Hakka — Hakka (simple and straightforward, often with beancurd instead of meat):

Mui Kong Restaurant
22 Murray Street (Food Alley); tel. 221 77 58

Plum Village Restaurant
16 Jalan Leban; tel. 458 90 05

Szechuan — The Szechuan specialities (hot and spicy) are particularly good in the following restaurants:

China Palace
#02–00 Wellington Building, 20 Bideford Road; tel. 235 13 78

Dragon City Szechuan Restaurant
Novotel Orchid Inn, 214 Dunearn Road; tel. 254 70 70

Golden Phoenix Szechuan Restaurant
Hotel Equatorial, 429 Bukit Timah Road; tel. 732 04 31

Liu Hsiang Lou Szechuan Restaurant
Allson Hotel, 101 Victoria Street; tel. 338 22 45

# Restaurants

Long Jiang Szechuan Restaurant
Crown Prince Hotel, 270 Orchard Road; tel. 732 11 11

Meisan Szechuan Restaurant
Royal Holiday Inn Crowne Plaza, 25 Scotts Road; tel. 731 79 96

Min Jiang Szechuan Restaurant
Goodwood Park Hotel, 22 Scotts Road; tel. 737 74 11

Omei Restaurant
Hotel Grand Central, 22 Cavenagh Road; tel. 737 27 35

Peking's speciality, the famous "Peking Duck", is served at the following restaurants:  Peking

Eastern Palace
Supreme House, Kramat Road

Shanghai Restaurant
Mayfair Hotel (Bird's nest soup a speciality)

Fut Sai Kai Vegetarian Restaurant  Vegetarian
143 Kitchener Road; tel. 298 03 36

Kingsland Vegetarian Restaurant
#03–43/46 People's Park Centre; tel. 534 18 46

Happy Realm Vegetarian Food
#03–16 Pearl Centre, Eu Tong Sen Street; tel. 222 61 41

Pine Tree Vegetarian Restaurant
51 Robinson Road; tel. 222 00 67

For meat and vegetable curries try the following:  Indian

Mayarani Restaurant
#01–09–13 Amara Hotel Shopping Centre, 165 Tanjong Pagar Road
Tel. 225 62 44

Orchard Mahajarah
Cuppage Terrace, 25 Cuppage Road; tel. 732 63 31

Rang Mahal
Hotel Imperial, 1 Jalan Rumbia; tel. 737 16 66

The Tandoor Restaurant
Holiday Inn Parkview, 11 Cavenagh Road; tel. 733 83 33

Ujagar Singh
7 St Gregory Place; tel. 336 15 86

Recommended restaurants with Indian vegetarian food:

Annalakshmi
#02–10 Excelsior Hotel & Shopping Complex, 5 Coleman Street
Tel. 339 30 07

Bombay Woodlands Restaurant
#B1–06 Forum Galleria, 583 Orchard Road; tel. 235 69 80

Komala Vilas Restaurant
76/78 Serangoon Road (Little India); tel. 293 69 80

## Restaurants

**Indonesian**

The following restaurants specialise in Indonesian food. This is very varied and includes specialities such as satay (small meat kebabs dipped in various sauces), "bami" and "nasi", dishes with noodles or rice:

Aziza's Restaurant
36 Emerald Hill Road; tel. 235 11 30

Bintang Timur
#02–08/13 Far East Plaza, Scotts Road; tel. 235 45 39

Sabar Menanti
62 Kandahar Street

**Japanese**

Japanese "shushi" is world-famous, and the fish dishes are also excellent.

Hisatomo Family Restaurant
#03–16 Raffles City Shopping Centre, 250 North Bridge Road
Tel. 339 11 00

Hoshigaoka
#03–45/46 Centrepoint, 175–180 Orchard Road; tel. 734 02 59

Inagiku Japanese Restaurant
Westin Stamford Hotel, 2 Stamford Road; tel. 338 85 85

Keyaki Japanese Restaurant
Pan Pacific Hotel, 7 Raffles Boulevard; tel. 336 81 11

**Korean**

Han Do Korean Restaurant
#05–01 Orchard Shopping Centre, 321 Orchard Road; tel. 235 84 51

The Korean Restaurant
#05–35 Specialist Centre, 277 Orchard Road; tel. 235 00 18

**Malay**

For Malay food (hot and spicy, often curried, but differing from Indian in the blends of spices) try the hawker centre at Newton Circus.

**Thai**

Thai food, best known for fish, meat and poultry dishes using plenty of fresh vegetables and subtle spices, is probably the lightest of all Eastern cuisines.

The following restaurants are worth recommending:

Bangkok Garden Thai Restaurant
Hotel Negara, 15 Claymore Drive; tel. 734 48 33

Cairnhill Thai Seafood Restaurant
#07–03 Cairnhill Place, 15 Cairnhill Road; tel. 733 66 66

Chao Phaya Thai Seafood Restaurant
#04–01 Holland Shopping Centre,
211 Holland Avenue; tel. 466 95 66

Parkway Thai Restaurant
#01–59/62 Centrepoint, 176 Orchard Road; tel. 235 18 33

**Nonya**

A composite of Chinese and Malay cooking, Nonya is probably the closest there is to a Singapore cuisine. Restaurants worth recommending include:

Bibis Restaurant
180 Orchard Road

Nonya & Baba
262 River Valley Road; tel. 734 13 82

Peranakan Inn
210 East Coast Road

All the big international hotels serve the usual Western dishes. — Western food

Singapore has a growing number of American fast-food outlets, including McDonald's, Pizza Hut, Burger King, and Kentucky Fried Chicken. — Fast food

See entry — Food and Drink

# Shopping

Singapore, the largest of market places for goods from all over the world and especially electronic and optical products from Asia, has made duty-free shopping its main attraction for tourists. There are dozens of malls and shopping centres, often each with over a hundred different shops, and streets lined with an unimaginable number of yet more shops.

The shopping centres are all air-conditioned and usually also contain banks and money changers (see Currency), hairdressers and beauticians, travel agents, airline offices, made-to-measure tailors and coffee houses.

Most of the department stores and specialist shops are on Orchard Road and Tanglin Road.

The range of goods on sale varies only slightly from one shopping centre to another so it pays to shop around and compare prices so as to be able to bargain more effectively. It is also wise to check on the price of optical and electonic goods before leaving home since they are not necessarily cheaper in Singapore.

The Singapore Tourist Promotion Board and the Consumers' Association operate a Good Retailers Scheme which qualifies shops to display the red Merlion GRS logo. The STPB is also trying to get all stores to price-tag their goods. However, stores displaying stickers saying "I'm tagged with a recommended price" allow bargaining, while those displaying "I'm tagged with a fixed price" mean what they say! — Good Retailers Scheme

Visitors may apply for a refund of the 3% Goods and Services Tax (GST) for goods worth S$500 or more bought in shops displaying the TAX REFUND sticker which indicates they are taking part in the GST Tourist Refund Scheme. — GST Tourist Refund

## Shopping Centres (selection)

Albert Complex, 60 Albert Street
Blanco Court, 585 North Bridge Road
Centrepoint, 176–184 Orchard Road
Cuppage Centre, 55 Cuppage Road
Far East Plaza, 14 Scotts Road
Forum Galleria, 583 Orchard Road
Funan Centre, 109 North Bridge Road
High Street Centre, 1 North Bridge Road
International Building, 300 Orchard Road
Liang Court Complex, 177 River Valley Road
Liat Towers, 541 Orchard Road
Marina Square, 6 Raffles Boulevard
Meridien Shopping Centre, 100 Orchard Road
Orchard Point, 160 Orchard Road
Paragon, 290 Orchard Road

## Shopping

Parkway Parade, 80 Marine Parade Road
Peninsula Plaza, 111 North Bridge Road
People's Park Centre, 101 Upper Cross Road
People's Park Complex, Eu Tong Sen Street
Plaza Singapura, 68 Orchard Road
Promenade, 300 Orchard Road
Raffles City, 250 North Bridge Road
Scotts, 6 Scotts Road
Serangoon, 320 Serangoon Road
Shaw Centre, 1 Scotts Road
Sim Lim Tower, 10 Jalan Besar
South Bridge Centre, 95 South Bridge Road
Specialists' Centre, 277 Orchard Road
Tanglin, 19 Tanglin Road
Wisma Atria, 435 Orchard Road
Robinsons, Centrepoint, Orchard Road
St Michael of Marks & Spencer, Centrepoint, Orchard Road
Tokyu, Marina Square, Raffles Boulevard
Yaohan, Plaza Singapura, Orchard Road, 80 Marine Parade Road

## Retailers (selection)

C K Tang Limited, 320 Orchard Road
Grand Classic Pte Ltd., 325 New Bridge Road
Halley's Department Store Pte Ltd., 1 Grange Road,
  #01–02/02–00 Orchard Building
Isetan (S) Limited:
  New Isetan Orchard, 435 Orchard Road, Wisma Atria
  Isetan Havelock, 407 Havelock/Outram Roads
  Isetan Katong, 80 Marine Parade Road, Parkway Parade
Klasse Department Store (Pte) Ltd., 304 Orchard Road, B 1–19 Lucky Plaza
Kong Ming Merchandise, 150 Orchard Road, #02–07/08 Orchard Plaza
Le Classique (Pte) Ltd., 2 Tanglin Road, #01–00 Le Classique House
branches:
  Century Park Sheraton, Nassim Hill
  Goodwood Park Hotel, 22 Scotts Road
  Jurong Bird Park, Jalan Ahmad Ibrahim, Jurong Town
  Sentosa, Jetty Road, Monorail Station
  Singapore Changi Airport, Departure Transit Hall – West Wing
  Singapore Changi Airport, Departure Transit Hall – East Wing
  Singapore Changi Airport, Viewing Gallery
Malaya Silk Store (Pte) Ltd., 321 Orchard Road,
  #01–01/02 Orchard Shopping Centre
Meitetsu Departmental Store (S) Pte Ltd., 402 Orchard Road,
  #02–07 18 Delfi Orchard
Metro (Pte) Ltd.
branches:
  Metro Grand at Scotts, Scotts Shopping Centre
  Metro Grand at Lucky Plaza, Lucky Plaza
  Metro Orchard, Royal Holiday Inn Building
  Metro Far East, Far East Plaza
  Metro Supreme, Supreme House
  Metro Golden Mile, The Plaza
Robinson & Co (S) Pte Ltd., 176 Orchard Road,
  #05–05 92 Centrepoint
Singapore Daimaru Pte Ltd., 177 River Valley Road, Liang Court
Tashing Co (Pte) Ltd., 1 Park Road, #05–02 People's Park Complex

## Department Stores

Bobby-O Department Store
Stamford Road; open: daily 10am–9pm

**Shopping**

C K Tang
Orchard Road, Dynasty Hotel; open: Mon.–Sat. 9.30am–8.30pm

Cortina
Colombo Street, North Bridge Road; open: daily 10.30am–7pm

Isetan
Apollo Hotel, Havelock Road; open: daily 10am–9pm

John Little
Plaza Singapura, Orchard Road; open: daily 10am–10pm

Klasse
Lucky Plaza, Orchard Road; open: daily 10am–10pm

Metro Bukhit Timah
Bukit Timah Plaza, Jalan Anak Bukit; open: daily 9.30am–10pm

Metro Golden Mile
Beach Road; open: daily 10am–9.30pm

Metro Orchard
Scotts Road; open: daily 9.30am–9.30pm

Metro Supreme
Supreme House, Penang Road; open: daily 10am–9.30pm

Metro Orchard
Scotts Road; open: daily 9.30am–9.30pm

Metro Supreme
Supreme House, Penang Road; open: daily 10am–9.30pm

O G Elite
Plaza Singapura, Orchard Road; open: Mon.–Sat. 11am–9.30pm

Robinson's
Specialist's Centre, Orchard Road
Open: Mon.–Wed. 9.45am–5.30pm, Thu., Sat. 9.45am–8.30pm,
Sun. 9.45am–5pm

Scott's Plus
Scott's Shopping Centre, Scott's Road; open: daily 10am–9pm

Yaohan Thomson
Upper Thomson Road, Thomson Plaza
Open: Mon.–Fri. 10am–10pm, Sat., Sun. 9.30am–10pm

## Specialist Shops (selection)

| | |
|---|---|
| Select Books, Tanglin Shopping Centre, Tanglin Road; tel. 737 82 95 | Books |
| Amir & Sons, Lucky Plaza; tel. 737 33 55<br>Oriental Carpet Palace, 163 H, Singapore Handicraft Centre, Tanglin Road; tel. 235 82 59<br>Hassan's Carpets, 177 Orchard Road; tel. 737 56 26 | Carpets |
| Chen Yee Shen, Oxford Road; tel. 737 11 74<br>Funan Art, Tanglin Shopping Centre, Tanglin Road; tel. 737 34 42<br>Beijing Antiques, Far East Plaza, Scott's Road; tel. 734 78 78<br>Ming Village, Pandan Road; tel. 265 77 11<br>Paul Art Gallery, Supreme House, Penang Road; tel. 338 12 17 | Chinese Crafts |

| | |
|---|---|
| Golden Million & Currency Agency, 11 Collyer Quay; tel. 223 10 44<br>Singapore Mint: see Currency | Coins |
| Centrepoint Complex, Mayfair Reptiles, Orchard Road; tel. 235 09 31<br>Far East Plaza, Scott's Road (several shops)<br>Far East Shopping Centre, Orchard Road, Les Must de Cartier; tel. 235 31 58<br>Goldhill Square, Gilbarto/Colnago; tel. 256 81 16<br>Lucky Plaza, Orchard Road (several shops)<br>Plaza Singapura, Orchard Road (several shops) | Reptile-skin/<br>leather goods |
| Katong Flower Shop, LG 12, Lower Ground Floor, Orchard Plaza,<br>Orchard Road; tel. 235 08 40 | Flowers |
| Lee Onn, 206/208 South Bridge Road; tel. 223 55 33<br>Eramanis, G14, Ground Floor, Tanglin Shopping Centre, Tanglin Road;<br>  tel. 737 32 46<br>Kampooli, G7, Ground Floor, Plaza Singapura, Orchard Road;<br>  tel. 336 13 81<br>CT Hoo, 27 Tanglin Road; tel. 235 93 43<br>Singapore Jewellery, Goodwood Hotel; tel. 737 71 68<br>Tin Sing Goldsmiths, 215/217 South Bridge Road; tel. 223 41 50 | Jewellery |
| Handloom House, 03–14 Orchard Towers; tel. 235 15 42<br>China Silk House, 111/113, 1st Floor, Tanglin Shopping Centre,<br>Tanglin Road; tel. 235 50 21 | Silk |
| De Silva, Tanglin Shopping Centre, Tanglin Road; tel. 737 85 28 | Silver |
| Tien Kee Brothers (Bali House), 23/27 Middle Road; tel. 338 18 03<br>Singapore Woodcraft, 318, 3rd Floor, Plaza Singapura,<br>Orchard Road; tel. 337 77 37<br>Singapore Souvenirs, B1–10 Lucky Plaza, Orchard Road;<br>  tel. 737 28 86<br>Seah Gallery, M5, Mezzanine Floor, Shangri-La; tel. 235 09 23 | Souvenirs/<br>Gifts |
| Fashion Tailors, 245 Orchard Road; tel. 737 40 43<br>Heero's Custom Tailors, G50 Lucky Plaza, Orchard Road;<br>  tel. 235 32 25<br>Shanghai Ladies' Dressmaker, 04–63 Lucky Plaza; tel. 235 20 02<br>Tat Bee Tailors, Lucky Plaza; tel. 235 33 66<br>Steven Bespoke Tailors, 146 Market Street, #01–16; tel. 222 71 36<br>Fatman, 02–27 Centrepoint, Orchard Road; tel. 737 94 72 | Tailors |

See also Tailormade clothing

## Sightseeing

Anyone with only one or two days to spend in Singapore and visiting the island for the first time would be well advised to go on an organised city tour. Singapore's tour operators offer a wide selection of general and special interest tours, including city tours of various kinds (see Travel Agencies), usually lasting between three and four hours. Information on these and other tours is also available from hotels and the Singapore Tourist Promotion Board (see Information).

Organised tours

Among the most popular are the Trishaw Tour, Founding Footsteps of Raffles, Sentosa Island, Jurong Bird Park and Ming Village, East Coast Tour, Junk Cruises, Zoo and Orchid Gardens, Singapore by Night, Round Island

◀ *Raffles City Shopping Centre*

**Sightseeing**

Tour, tours of hawker stalls, jungle walks, visits to rubber plantations and excursions to Malacca and Johor Bahru.

Visitors who prefer to go on their own can seek the advice of the Singapore Tourist Promotion Board or follow one of the itineraries outlined below (places in **bold** appear in the A–Z section).

| | |
|---|---|
| Boat trips | See entry |
| Stopovers | Anyone stopping over between flights for more than four hours can take advantage of the free city tours from the airport courtesy of the Singapore Tourist Promotion Board (see Air Travel). |
| Singapore Explorer bus ticket | The Singapore Explorer bus ticket is a one-day (S$5) or three-day (S$12) Singapore Bus Service pass for unlimited travel anywhere on the island, and obtainable from hotels, SBS travel centres or SBS Passenger Service (205 Braddell Road; tel. 287 27 27). The Explorer Bus Map, available at the same time, suggests various routes –- Historic Singapore, The Chinese Influence, The Temple Route, and Flora and Fauna are among the most interesting – and gives an account of the sights along the way. |
| Singapore Trolley | The historic Singapore trolley, recently revived to suit the tourist, runs from 9am to 10pm along a route designed to go from one sight to another with the opportunity of getting off at any of the 22 stops or staying on to the end of the line and hearing the whole of the guided commentary. Tickets, which include discounts at local shops and nightspots, can be bought from hotels or on board the trolley. |
| Trolley route | The trolleys take the following route (places in **bold** appear in the A–Z section, those in brackets are easily reached on foot from that particular stop): |

Gleneagles Hospital (Botanic Gardens) – ANA Hotel – Orchard Hotel (Tanglin shopping centre, Forum Galleria, Orchard Towers, Shaw Centre, Far East shopping centre, Liat Towers, Delfi Orchard) – Dynasty Hotel (Tangs, Scotts shopping centre, Far East Shopping Plaza, Lucky Plaza, Wisma Atria shopping centre, The Promenade, Paragon shopping centre) – Orchard Plaza (Centrepoint, Specialist's Centre, Orchard shopping centre, Orchard Emerald, Peranakan Plaza, Cuppage Centre, Cuppage Plaza, Orchard Point, Orchard Plaza, Istana, Meridien shopping centre, Plaza Singapore) – Plaza by the Park (**Fort Canning Park**, **National Museum**) – Westin Plaza (**Raffles Hotel**, **Raffles City**, War Memorial Park, Saint Andrew's Cathedral) – Pan Pacific Hotel (**Marina Square**) – Tokyu (Satay Club) – Lim Bo Seng Memorial (Fullerton Building, **Empress Place**, **Merlion Park**, Lim Bo Seng Memorial, **Padang**, **Victoria Concert Hall & Theatre**, Parliament House, **Supreme Court**, City Hall, **Armenian Church**) – Telok Ayer Market (**Telok Ayer Street**, Festival Market, Clifford Pier, Harbour Cruise) – Sri Mariamman Temple (**Chinatown**, **Sri Mariamman Temple**, Chinaman Scholar Gallery) – 51 Neil Road (Tanjong Pagar Conservation Area) – Pearl's Centre (**People's Park Centre**, Chinatown Point) – **Singapore River** – Capitol Theatre – YMCA – Orchard School – Orchard MRT – Boulevard Hotel – Marco Polo Hotel – Botanic Gardens

# Chinatown

Any visit to this Chinese quarter of the city requires time for a leisurely stroll with a chance simply to stand and stare, explore or go shopping in the Kreta Ayer Complex (**Markets**), **Change Alley**, People's Park Centre or **Telok Ayer Street**. A quick look at the map will make it possible to combine sauntering with sightseeing, whilst snacking or dining at the many hawkers and Chinese restaurants along the way.

**Sightseeing**

*Modern fountain sculpture*

The sights particularly worth seeing are the **Sri Mariamman Hindu Temple**, Singapore's oldest temple of its kind, with nearby in Pagoda Street, the Jamae Mosque, completed in 1835. The **Thian Hok Keng Temple** is Singapore's oldest Chinese temple. En route to the most important of the Malay Muslim shrines, **Keramat Habib Noh** in Palmer Road, you pass the Al Abrar Mosque in Telok Ayer Street, an elegant Indian mosque dating from the mid-19th c.

## Around Empress Place

There is plenty to see in this quarter north of the **Singapore River**. Grouped around the starting point of **Empress Place**, opposite **Merlion Park** and its emblem of Singapore, are a number of sights including the **Victoria Memorial Hall & Victoria Theatre**. Go for a stroll along Queen Elizabeth Walk or in **Padang**. Nearby Parliament House, Singapore's City Hall, built originally as a merchant's home in 1825, and the neighbouring **Supreme Court** make this area Singapore's seat of government. After taking in **Saint Andrew's Cathedral**, the **Chinese Chamber of Commerce** and the **Armenian Church** head for the lofty landmark of **Raffles City**, Singapore's latest business and hotel skyscraper. And perhaps end up opposite with a gin sling in the legendary **Raffles Hotel**.

## Around Fort Canning Park

After visiting the **National Museum** and Art Gallery you can get to know **Fort Canning Park** and its Van Kleef Aquarium before moving on to **Chettiar's Hindu Temple** and the **Chesed-el Synagogue**, neither of which are very far away, then look in on the **Tan Si Chong Su Temple** on Magazine Road.

**Sightseeing**

*On every tourist's list – Singapore's Chinatown*

## Around Little India

Take a bus or a taxi to get to **Little India**. Centred on Serangoon Road, it has its Muslim shopping district around **Arab Street**, with the **Sultan Mosque** and **Hajjah Fatimah Mosque** close by, while Serangoon Road itself leads out of town to the **Sri Srinivasa Perumal Temple** and the **Temple of 1000 Lights**. About 9km/5½ miles north of the centre is the **Siong Lim Monastery**, Singapore's largest and probably finest Buddhist temple.

## Around Orchard Road

Singapore's main shopping street is also one of its principal traffic arteries and easy to get to by taxi, trolley or bus. From here it is but a relatively short detour via **Emerald Hill Road** to a carefully renovated residential quarter and then anyone wanting to recover from the exertions of shopping can relax with a stroll in the **Botanic Gardens**, one of the most attractive of the city's shady tropical parks.

## Swimming

There are plenty of opportunities for swimming and water sports on **Sentosa Island**, the **Saint John's Islands**, **Changi Beach** and the **East Coast Park Lagoon** (see also Beaches).

## Singapore's Islands

Singapore's 54 islands, most of them to the south, lend themselves to excursions. **Sentosa Island**, which can be reached by cable car from **Mount Faber** and the World Trade Centre, offers theme parks, golf, swimming, and museums and, like **Saint John's Islands** and **Kusu Island**, is also served by ferries from the Singapore Cruise Centre at the World Trade Centre.

## Nearby Attractions

For anyone who has time to spare after touring the city there are several other places worth seeing in the north and the west of the main island, and easy to get to by bus or with a taxi or hire car (see Car Rental, Public Transport).

Heading west from the city, you first pass **Keppel Harbour**, Singapore's port. Further on **Haw Par Villa**, formerly Tiger Balm Gardens, offers an insight into Chinese mythology, then about 15½ miles from the city centre comes **Jurong Town**, with its Chinese and Japanese Gardens and Bird Park. For anyone in need of a break from so much flora and fauna the nearby Singapore Science Centre (see **Jurong Town**) makes science highly accessible to adults and children alike.

Attractions in the north of the island with a theme based on the natural world include **MacRitchie Reservoir**, **Bukit Timah Nature Reserve**, Singapore's Zoological Gardens at **Seletar Reservoir**, and the **Mandai Orchid Gardens**, among the finest of their kind in the world.
The beautifully landscaped **Kranji War Memoral** further to the north is dedicated to the Allied troops who fell in 1942.

## Excursions further afield

A number of tour operators runs trips of one day or more to neighbouring Malaysia and Indonesia.
For information consult the Singapore Tourist Promotion Board (see Information) or the sections on Bus Trips, Ferries, and Rail Travel.

Places worth seeing include **Johor Bahru** and all it has to offer, **Kota Tinggi** and **Malacca**. Tours also run to the Indonesian islands of Batam and Bintan, with its principal town **Tanjung Pinang**, or you can take the ferry. Information is available from the Indonesian Tourist Promotion Office (see Information).

A bird's-eye view of the Singapore skyline is a fascinating experience and anyone who misses the view when arriving at Changi Airport can consider a pleasure flight in a light plane or helicopter. For further information ask at the hotel front desk or contact:

Singapore from the air

Singapore Aerospace Engineering
Charter Operations Department
Seletar Airbase; tel. 481 05 46

## Souvenirs

Although Singapore produces no genuine souvenirs of its own it ranks with Hong Kong as the largest market in the Far East for antiques (see entry), curios and art craftwork from all over the world but especially Asia.
For the addresses of shopping centres, department stores and specialist shops see Shopping.

## Sport

The Singapore Sports Council runs the 60,000 seater National Stadium with facilities for athletics, squash, tennis and golf, plus a sports hall, and is responsible for 3 more halls, 6 athletics centres, 34 multi-purpose pitches, 23 swimming baths, 8 netball pitches, 67 tennis courts, 38 squash courts and several fitness centres.

## Sport

Many hotels also have their own sporting and keep-fit facilities, some of them free of charge.

**Badminton**

Badminton Hall, Guillemard Road; tel. 245 12 22

**Bowling**

Bowling Centre, Hyatt Singapore Hotel; tel. 737 55 11
Jackie's Bowl, 542B, East Coast Road; tel. 241 65 19
Jackie's Bowl, 8 Grange Road; tel. 737 47 44
Jurong Family Bowl, Yuan Ching Road; tel. 265 54 33
Kallang Bowl, 5 Stadium Walk; tel. 345 05 45
Pasir Panjang Bowl, Pasir Panjang Road; tel. 775 55 55
Plaza Bowl, 3rd floor, Textile Centre, Jalan Sultan; tel. 292 48 21
Starbowl, 5th floor, Peace Centre; tel. 338 14 21

**Flying**

Republic of Singapore Flying Club, East Camp; tel. 481 05 02

**Golf**

Singapore's many golf courses and its love of golf hark back to the Colonial era. The Singapore Tourist Promotion Board (see Information) also publishes a brochure "Golf in Singapore". Golf courses which allow visitors on payment of the green fee include the following:

Changi Golf Club, Netheravon Road; tel. 545 51 33
Jurong Country Club, Science Centre Road; tel. 560 56 55
Keppel Club, Bukit Chermin; tel. 273 55 22
Seletar Country Club, Seletar Airbase; tel. 481 47 45
Sembawang Golf Club, Sembawang Road; tel. 257 06 42
Sentosa Golf Club, Sentosa Island; tel. 275 00 22
Singapore Island Country Club, Upper Thomson Road; tel. 459 22 22
Warren Golf Club, Folkestone Road; tel. 777 65 33

**Gymnastics**

Clark Hatch Physical Fitness Centre, Marco Polo
Dynami Fitness Centre, Meridien Hotel
Fitness International, Pavilion Inter-Conti
Hyatt Fitness Centre, Hyatt Hotel
Hydra-Fitness Asia, Sheraton Hotel
National Stadium Gymnasium, Kallang; tel. 345 12 22
Nautilus Fitness Centre, York Hotel
Oasis Sports and Leisure Club, Pan Pacific Hotel

**Horse racing**

Bukit Turf Club, Bukit Timah Road
See A–Z, Turf Club; tel. 469 36 11

**Horse riding**

Green Dale Riding School; tel. 460 22 09
Saddle Club, Bukit Turf Club, Bukit Timah Road
See A–Z, Turf Club; tel. 466 27 82
Singapore Polo Club, Thomson Road; tel. 256 45 30

**Sailing/yacht clubs**

Changi Sailing Club, Netheravon Road; tel. 445 12 98
East Coast Sailing Centre; tel. 449 51 18
Ponggol Boatel; tel. 280 64 44
Republic of Singapore Yacht Club, Jalan Buroh; tel. 265 09 31
Singapore Armed Forces Yacht Club, Seletar Air Base; tel. 481 01 84

**Scuba diving**

Singapore Sub-Aqua Club; tel. 445 62 53

**Squash**

Alexandra Park, Bedford Roads; tel. 473 72 36
Changi Squash Courts, Cranwell Road; tel. 445 29 44
Clementi Recreation Centre, 12 West Coast Walk; tel. 747 889 66
East Coast Recreation Centre, East Coast Parkway; tel. 449 05 41
Farrer Park, Rutland Road; tel. 251 41 66
National Stadium, Kallang; tel. 348 12 58
Singapore Squash Centre, Fort Canning Rise; tel. 337 42 80

**Tailormade clothing**

| | |
|---|---|
| Alexandra Park, Royal Road; tel. 63 72 36<br>Changi Tennis Court, Cranwell Road; tel. 445 29 41<br>East Coast Park Lagoon; tel. 442 59 66<br>Farrer Park, Rutland Road; tel. 293 16 64 | Tennis |
| Ponggol Boatel, Ponggol Point; tel. 481 00 31/2 | Waterskiing |
| East Coast Sailing Centre; tel. 449 51 18<br>See also A–Z, East Coast Park Lagoon, Sentosa Island | Windsurfing |

## Tailormade clothing

In Singapore you can get any kind of clothing made-to-measure, usually by Sikh tailors who seem to have cornered this market for hand-tailored garments at reasonable prices.

Many hotels, especially the larger ones, have excellent ladies' and gents' tailors in-house, albeit at prices to match. The workmanship of the countless tailors in tourist areas and the shops along Coleman Street, Selegie Road, North Bridge Road, Orchard Road and Tanglin Road is no less good, although the names of the best ones are usually passed on by word of mouth. For a brief selection see Shopping (Specialist Shops).

A look in the shop window will give you some idea of the quality of the end product, and if there is a problem about what model to have ask to see one of the international fashion magazines usually on display. Once you have been measured and have placed an order expect to leave a deposit in the order of 20% of the price. Although many tailors can deliver within 24 hours allow three days for a suit and certainly no less than two in order to have at least one more fitting before accepting the final garment.

Buying tailor-made clothes

Every good tailor has a reasonable selection of fabrics of a quality and pattern well suited to European fashions, and many of them contain silk in

Fabrics

*Made to measure: a tailor's shop in Singapore*

**Taxis**

varying amounts to improve their wearing qualities. Pure Chinese or Thai silk lends itself to men's shirts and women's evening-wear. Chinese silk is the more expensive of the two but also more crease-resistant.

## Taxis

Singapore has over 10,000 air-conditioned taxis, all under seven years old. They can be hailed on the street, picked up from taxi ranks, or ordered by phone (24-hour phoneline; tel. 452 55 55/474 77 07). The London-style cabs are particularly roomy and can take up to five people (information from TIBS Radiophone; tel. 481 12 11).

Fares

All taxis have meters and these must be used at all times. The initial fare is S$2.40 and covers the first 1.5km/1 mile, with 10 cents for every 240 metres thereafter. There is a 50% surcharge between midnight and 6am, and a S$1 surcharge on all London cabs.

Tipping/Smoking

Singapore is one country where tipping is frowned upon! And anyone caught smoking in an air-conditioned taxi is liable to a fine or even imprisonment.

Long-distance travel by taxi

A taxi can be a faster and more comfortable way of getting to Malaysia than going by bus (see Bus Trips). For further information contact the Malaysia Tourist Promotion Board (see Information).

## Telecommunications

Singapore has a state-of-the-art telephone service, linked to the international network by satellite and underwater cable. Many hotels have international direct dialling (IDD), and this is also available at the General Post Office (see Post) and Comcentre, as well as from the many phonecard and credit card telephones at post offices and around the city. The number for the international operator is 104, but there are also several "Home Country Direct" lines to countries such as Australia, the United States and the United Kingdom.

When making an international call be sure to remember the time difference.

International dialling codes

To call Singapore from abroad dial the international code followed by 65 (no area code required) and the subscriber's number. To call abroad from Singapore dial 005 followed by your own country code (Australia 61, Canada 1, Eire 359, New Zealand 64, South Africa 27, United Kingdom 44, United States 1). The access code for Malaysia is 109.

Enquiries

Local enquiries: tel. 103. International enquiries: tel. 104.

Charges

Calls within Singapore are free, even from hotels, but from public telephones they cost 10 cents for 3 minutes. Phonecards come in five denominations of S$2, S$5, S$10, S$20 and S$50 and are available from post offices, phonecard agents and Singapore Telecom outlets. Hotels normally add 20% for IDD calls.

Telegrams, faxes, telexes

Telegrams, faxes and telexes come under Singapore Telecom which has separate facilities from the post offices. Most hotels also have their own faxing facilities. Telegrams (normal or urgent rate) can be sent over the phone (tel. 533 02 34) and from Telecom's Telephone House, 35 Robinson Road.

## Time

Singapore Standard Time is 8 hours ahead of Greenwich Mean Time, 15 hours ahead of Los Angeles, 12 hours ahead of New York, 2 hours behind

Sydney and 4 hours behind Auckland. There is no change for Summer Time.

## Tipping

Tipping is expressly discouraged in Singapore, and no tip for special services rendered should be more than 50 cents–S$2. Most hotels and restaurants include a 10% service charge in the bill.

## Toilets

Singapore's toilets are well up to European standards, and there are plenty of public toilets, all regularly checked by health inspectors.

## Travel Agencies

There are about 400 officially licensed travel agencies in Singapore and travel can be booked to anywhere in the world. Most deal with local as well as international travel and tour operators, and the competition is fierce, so it pays to shop around.

They are listed under Travel Agencies in the Yellow Pages. Any complaints about their services should be directed to the Singapore Tourist Promotion Board (see Information).

## Travel Documents

All persons entering Singapore must have a passport valid for at least six months beyond date of entry or other internationally recognised travel document. Visas are not required for British, Commonwealth or United States citizens entering Singapore in transit or for social visits of up to 90 days. Visitors coming in as tourists are given a 14-day social visit pass on arrival, and if they want to stay longer they can then apply to the Immigration Department. — Passports/visas

Singapore Immigration Department, 7th Floor, South Bridge Centre, South Bridge Road; tel. 532 28 77. Open: Mon.–Fri. 8am–5pm, Sat. 8am–1pm. — Immigration department

Vaccination certificates are only required if the visitor is coming from an area affected with yellow fever or cholera, or has visited one within the previous 6 days (see also Health Care). — Vaccinations

Anyone expecting to arrive by sea in their own boat should check on entry formalities beforehand with the Port of Singapore Authority (tel. 271 22 11) or the overseas offices of the Singapore Tourist Promotion Board (see Information). — Arrivals by sea

## Weather Forecasts

Weather forecasts are broadcast at the end of television news bulletins and published in the daily papers.

**When to Go**

Tide tables and detailed shipping weather forecasts are provided by the daily press (see Newspapers and Periodicals), the Singapore Port Authority (tel. 271 22 11), and the Tourist Promotion Board (see Information).

## When to Go

The best time to visit Singapore is from late March to June, outside the monsoon season. The weather can also be very pleasant during the north-east monsoon (December to March) and the south-west monsoon (June to September) since the rain is only for a few hours each day and the skies soon clear again, although it can get very sultry and oppressively hot.

Singapore is only 135km/52½ miles from the Equator so temperatures average about 30°C/86°F during the day, and only slightly less at night.

Climate

See Facts and Figures

## Youth Hostels

Singapore has no youth hostels as such but the Singapore Tourist Promotion Board (see Information) does keep a list of recommended accommodation for travellers on a limited budget, and there is always the YWCA and YMCA.

YMCA International House, 1 Orchard Road; tel. 336 60 00
Metropolitan YMCA, 60 Stevens Road; tel. 737 77 55
YWCA Hostel, 6/8 Fort Canning Road; tel. 336 12 12

## Useful Telephone Numbers at a Glance

| | |
|---|---|
| Police (freephone) | 999 |
| Fire (freephone) | 995 |
| Ambulance (freephone) | 995 |
| AA 24-hour breakdown service | 748 99 11 |
| Airlines | |
| British Airways | 253 84 44 |
| Malaysian Airways | 336 67 77 |
| Quantas | 737 37 44 |
| Singapore Airlines | 223 88 88 |
| Automobile Association of Singapore | 737 24 44 |
| Diplomatic missions | |
| Australia | 737 93 11 |
| Canada | 225 63 63 |
| Ireland | 733 21 80 |
| New Zealand | 235 99 66 |
| South Africa | 339 33 19 |
| United Kingdom | 473 93 33 |
| United States | 338 02 51 |

## Useful Telephone Numbers at a Glance

Hospitals
   Alexandra Hospital                              63 52 22
   Mount Elizabeth Hospital              737 26 66
   National University Hospital         779 55 55
   NUH Dialysis Unit                        259 92 17
   Singapore General Hospital        222 33 22
   Tao Payoh Hospital                      256 04 11

Immigration Department                     532 28 77

Information
   Flight information                       1800 542 44 22/542 69 88
   Train station                              222 51 65

Taxis
   24-hour phoneline                      452 55 55/474 77 07
   TIBS Radiophone                        481 12 11

Tourist information
   Singapore Tourist Promotion Board    339 66 22
   STPB Information Centre             1800 334 13 35/334 13 36

Telecommunications
   Telegrams                                533 02 34
   Directory enquiries: local               103
                      international       104

Dialling codes: Singapore               65
                Malaysia access code      109
International operator                       104
International Direct Dialling           005

Weather
   Weather service                         542 77 88
   Sea weather report                    271 22 11

# Index

**A**bdul Gaffoor Mosque 41
Agriculture, Fisheries 25
Air Travel 102
   Airlines 104
   Airport 102
Alkaff Mansion 41
Antiques 105
Arab Street 41
Armenian Church 41
Around Empress Place 149
Around Fort Canning
   Park 149
Around Little India 150
Around Orchard Road 150
Art 20

**B**anks 112
Beaches 106
Bird Park 42, 60
Boat Cruises 106
Botanic Gardens 42
Bugis Street 43
Bukit Timah Nature
   Reserve 44
Bus trips 107
Butterfly Park 44

**C**amping 107
Car rental 107
Central Beach 44
Central Park 44
Changi Airport 44
Changi Beach 45
   Prisoners Chapel 46
Chemists 108
Chemists and
   Pharmacies 126
Chesed-el Synagogue 46
Chettiars Hindu
   Temple 46
Chinatown 48, 148
Chinese Chamber of
   Commerce 50
Chinese Garden 51
Chinese Street Opera 108
Cinema 109
Clarke Quay 51
Clifford Pier 51
Clothing 109
Concerts 110
Conduct and Behaviour 109
Coralarium 51
Crocodile Farm 51
Crocodile Paradise 52
Culture 18
Cuppage Road Market 52

Currency 110
Customs Regulations 113

**D**epartment Stores 144
Diplomatic
   Representation 113
Disabled Access 114
Drugs 114

**E**ast Coast Park
   Lagoon 52
Economy 22
Education system 19
Electricity 115
Elizabeth Walk 53
Emerald Hill 53
Emergency Services 115
Employment policy 25
Empress Place 53
Events and Festivals 115
Excursions further
   afield 151

**F**acts and Figures 7
Famous People 28
Ferries 120
Festivals 120
Fish Markets 53
Flight Packages 105
Folklore 120
Food and Drink 120
Fort Canning Park 54
Fort Siloso 54
Fuk Tak Ch'i Temple 55

**G**eneral 7
Getting to Singapore 124
Geylang Serai 55

**H**ajjah Fatima Mosque 56
Haw Par Villa 56
Health Care 125
High Street 57
History 32
Hong San See Temple 57
Hospitals 126
Hotels 127
House of Tan Yeok Nee 58

**I**ndustry 23
Information 129
Insectarium 58
Insurance 130

**J**apanese Garden 58

Johor Bahru 58
   Abu Bakar Mosque 58
   Istana Besar 59
   Istana Garden 59
   Kota Tinggi 59
   Kukup 59
   Royal Mausoleum 59
Jurong Town 60
   Bird Park 60
   Chinese Garden &
      Japanese Garden 60
   Jurong Crocodile
      Paradise 61
   Singapore Science
      Centre 61

**K**elongs 62
Keppel Harbour 62
Keramat Habib Noh 62
Kong Meng San Phor Kark
   62
Kota Tinggi 63
Kranji War Memorial 63
Kuan Yin Temple 64
Kusu Island 64
   Tua Pek Kong Temple 64

**L**anguage 12, 130
Libraries and Archives 130
Little India 65
   Abdul Gaffoor
      Mosque 65
Lost Property 131

**M**acRitchie Reservoir 66
Malacca 66
   A Famosa 67
   Bukit China 68
   Cheng Hoon Teng
      Temple 68
   Chinatown 69
   Christ Church 69
   Light and Sound
      Show 69
   St Paul's Church 70
   Stadthuys 70
   Tranquera Mosque 70
Malaysia 71
Mandai Orchid Gardens 71
Marina Bay 71
Maritime Museum 72
Markets 72, 132
Measurements 131
Medical Facilities 126
Memorial Hall and Victoria
   Theatre 74

# Index

Merlion Park 74
Ming Village 74
Motoring 131
Mount Faber 76
Museums 131
Musical Fountain 76

**N**agore Durgha Shrine 76
National Museum 77
National Stadium 77
National University 78
Nearby Attractions 151
Newspapers and
 Periodicals 132
Nightlife 132

**O**pening Times 132

**P**adang 78
Parks and Nature
 Reserves 133
Pasar Malam 79
Pasir Ris Beach Park 79
Peranakan Museum 79
Peranakan Place 79
Perumal Temple 79
Photography and Film 133
Population 12
Post 134
Practical Information 102
Public Holidays 134
Public Transport 136
Pulau Hantau 79

**Q**ueen Elizabeth Walk 79

**R**acecourse 80
Radio and Television 137
Raffles City 80
Raffles Hotel 80
Raffles Monument 80
Raffles Place 83
Rail Travel 138
Religion 14
Religious Services 138
Representation in
 Singapore 113

Restaurants 139
Retailers 144

**S**TPB Offices Abroad 129
Saint Andrew's
 Cathedral 83
Saint John's Islands 83
Sakya Muni Buddha Gaya
 Temple 83
Science Center 83
Seletar Reservoir 84
Sentosa Island 84
 Terminal 85
 Musical Fountain 86
 Sentosa Riverboat 86
 Maritime Museum 86
 Coralarium 86
 Dari Laut 86
 Art Centre 87
 Wax Museum 99
 Fort Siloso 87
 Butterfly Park 87
 Rare Stone Museum 87
 Underwater World 88
 Asian Cultural Village 88
Serangoon Market 88
Shopping 143
Shopping Centres 143
Sightseeing 147
Siloso Beach 88
Singapore River 89
Singapore Science
 Centre 89
Singapore Tourist
 Promotion Board 129
Singapore from A to Z 41
Singapore in Quotations 37
Singapore's Islands 150
Siong Lim See
 Monastery 90
Sisters Island 90
Souvenirs 151
Specialist Shops 146
Sport 151
Sri Mariamman Hindu
 Temple 90

Sri Srinivassa Perumal
 Temple 92
State 21
Substation 92
Sultan Mosque 93
Sultan's Tomb 93
Supreme Court 93
Swimming 150

**T**ailormade clothing 153
Tan Si Chong Su Temple 95
Tang Dynasty City 94
Tanjong Pagar Road 94
Tanjung Pinang 95
Taxis 154
Telecommunications 154
Telok Ayer Street 95
 Telok Ayer Market 96
Temple of 1000 Lights 96
Thian Hok Keng Temple 97
Tiger Balm Gardens 97
Time 154
Tipping 155
Toilets 155
Tourism 23
Trade 23
Transport 25
Travel Agencies 155
Travel Documents 155
Tua Pek Kong Temple 98
Turf Club 98

**U**nderwater World 99
Useful Telephone Numbers
 at a Glance 156

**V**an Kleef Aquarium 99
Victoria Memorial Hall &
 Victoria Theatre 99

**W**ax Museum 87
Weather Forecasts 155
When to Go 156

**Y**outh Hostels 156

**Z**oological Gardens 99

**Imprint**

86 illustrations, 3 ground plans, 6 drawings, 4 general maps, 1 transport map, 1 large map (at the end of the book)

Original German text: Jürgen Dauth
Editorial work: Baedeker, Stuttgart
Revised text: Heiner Gstaltmayr
General direction: Dr Peter Baumgarten, Baedeker Stuttgart

Cartography: Christoph Gallus, Hohberg; Franz Kaiser, Sindelfingen; Gert Oberländer, Munich; Archiv für Flaggenkunde Ralf Stelter, Hattigen

Source of Illustrations: Beck 11, Dauth 37, Gstaltmayr 4, Imhof 24, Singapore Airlines 1, Singapore Tourist Promotion Board 3, Storto 1, Uthoff 5

Original English Translation: James Hogarth
Revised text: Brenda Ferris, Julie Waller
Editorial work: Margaret Court

2nd English edition 1995

© Baedeker Stuttgart
Original German edition 1994

© 1995 Jarrold and Sons Ltd
English language edition worldwide

© 1995 The Automobile Association: United Kingdom and Ireland

Published in the United States by:
Macmillan Travel
A Simon & Schuster Macmillan Company
15 Columbus Circle
New York, NY 10023

Macmillan is a registered trademark of Macmillan, Inc.

Distributed in the United Kingdom by the Publishing Division of the Automobile Association, Fanum House, Basingstoke, Hampshire RG21 2EA

All rights reserved. No part of this publication may be reproduced, stored in a retrieval system or transmitted in any form by any means – electronic, photocopying, recording or otherwise – unless the written permission of the publisher has been obtained.

Licensed user: Mairs Geographischer Verlag GmbH & Co., Ostfildern-Kemnat bei Stuttgart

The name *Baedeker* is a registered trademark

A CIP catalogue record of this book is available from the British Library

Printed in Italy by G. Canale & C.S.p.A – Borgaro T.se –Turin

ISBN 0–02–860489–X US and Canada
       0 7495 1102 8 UK